THE PULSE OF WANG WEI

Translated by David Du

Edited by Scot MacKenzie Jamieson

The Pulse of Wang Wei
Translated by David Du

MacKenzie Publishing
Halifax, Nova Scotia
June 2019
ISBN: 978-1-927529-70-6

Edited by Scot MacKenzie Jamieson

Front cover image: Wang Wei's "Snow on the Yangtze"
Chuan Wang Wei "Changjiang Snow Map" (partial), Honolulu (Honolulu) art collection (public domain)

Back cover image: The stone plaque indicates that it is the burial site of Wang Wei and his mother and the location of a temple built by Wang Wei roughly 1300 years ago, where he would feed the wild deer, which he loved. The Ginkgo (a very long-lived tree genus) beside the plaque was planted by Wang Wei. Presently this site is a town known as Wangchuan.

Contact David at: dudavid5326@gmail.com

MacKenzie Publishing

XINJIANG UYGHUR A. R.
Urumqi
TIBET A. R.
Lhasa
GANSU
Lanzhou
QINGHAI
Xining
NINGXIA
HUI A. R.
Yinchuan
INNER MONGOLIA A. R.
Hohhot
HEILONGJIANG
Harbin
JILIN
Changchun
LIAONING
Shenyang
BEIJING
TIANJIN
HEBEI
Shijiazhuang
SHANXI
Taiyuan
SHAN-
DONG
Jinan
SHAANXI
Xi'an
HENAN
Zhengzhou
JIANG-
SU
Nanjing
SHANGHAI
ANHUI
Hefei
HUBEI
Wuhan
SICHUAN
Chengdu
ZHE-
JIANG
Hangzhou
HUNAN
Changsha
JIANGXI
Nanchang
FUJIAN
Fuzhou
GUIZHOU
Guiyang
YUNNAN
Kunming
GUANGXI
ZHUANG A. R.
Nanning
GUANGDONG
Guangzhou
HONG KONG
MACAU
TAIWAN
HAINAN
Haikou

EDITOR'S NOTE

This book of poetry has the scope and colour of a novel, full of history, battles and intrigues, and the seductions of both the worldly and the spiritual. Acute observations on many social levels, and the warm friendships of a large hearted poet are here, and the excitements of a fantasy novel as well – a trip to a world remote in time, and for westerners, place. They touch the pulse, as David likes to say.

Scot MacKenzie Jamieson

ACKNOWLEDGEMENTS

To translate from one language to another is a great challenge, especially to translate from ancient Chinese into modern English. Is it a fitting punishment for the builders' pride in their fine tower of Babel, the great confusion of language? When I started to do this work, a friend gave me a book of old Chinese poetry translated by Arthur Waley. I saw that many words in his book didn't match the poet's meaning, so I made a decision to translate some ancient Chinese poems myself, which developed into taking a long journey—almost two and half years. I finished 200 pieces of poetry, all written by China's famous Wang Wei.

Through this time of assiduous effort, I was greatly helped by Mr. Scot MacKenzie Jamieson, who kindly edited my work. He is knowledgeable about English poetry, though having no Chinese. He is my indispensable counterpart, and without his help, I wouldn't have fulfilled my ambition. I also thank Cathy MacKenzie for her skill and co-operation.

I have a bachelor's degree in Chinese Literature that helped me to have a deeper understanding of ancient Chinese. I write both Chinese and English poetry, which was of much practical assistance in translating the ancient Chinese works. Last year, I went to China and visited Wang Wei's homeland and long term abode, Wang Chuan (River Wang), searching for the inspiration to better understand him.

I thank heaven for this work. I know many people have translated Wang Wei's poetry, but in my translations, I want to offer new interpretations and expressions, stemming directly from the originals.

David Du
Halifax, Nova Scotia, Canada
June 2019

INTRODUCTION

Ancient Chinese Poetry is divided into two periods, the unpatterned and the patterned. The unpatterned period of poetry belongs to the time before the Tang Dynasty (approx. 600 AD to 900 AD). In this period, all the poetry rhymes, but the poems don't express their content in the later, more complex traditional style of the Tang Dynasty.

During the Tang period, poetry changed. Poetic patterns were established and agreement was reached to focus on a 2-pattern style—in Chinese they call this Lv and Jue, specific forms of Classical Chinese verse, and the tongue pattern is different from modern Chinese.

Unlike English, Chinese has the feature of tongue patterns. This is called Pinyin in Chinese and is the Chinese pronunciation (tongue) system. In short, the identical word can have more than one meaning, depending on the inflection or tone, or as they say, tongue, that is used. The four tongues of modern Chinese are: Level, Rising, Departing, and Entering. In ancient Chinese, poetry was categorized only into Level (ping in Chinese) and Oblique (ze in Chinese).

However, the pattern in which Level and Oblique tones occur in one line is often the inverse of that of the line next to it. Complexity indeed results. For example:

The basic pattern is: the first line is ping ping ze ze ping, and the next line is ze ze ping ping ze. However, sometimes there are exceptions to this principle. For example, in "Deer Thicket," the first line is ping ping ze ze ping, but the second line is not exactly inverse: ze ping ping ze ze.

Deer Thicket
Wang Wei
(in the Tang Dynasty's ancient Chinese poetic style)

Kong Shan Bu Jian Ren
Dan Wen Ren Yu Xiang

Fan Jing Ru Shen Lin
Fu Zhao Qing Tai Shang

The "Kong" line is spoken with the Level tongue, and the "Dan" line is spoken with the Oblique tongue, and so on, and while the last words in the first and third lines are unrhymed, the second and fourth lines must rhyme. And the rhymes must be the same—in this case, the rhyme in the second and fourth lines is the "ang" sound. This style is called Jue or Wu Jue in Chinese. This means the 5-word, 4-line verse that is seen above in "Deer Thicket."

Sometimes the first line will rhyme, too. A Chinese "word" is a Chinese written character, which is not exactly one English word, but is one Chinese word.

The other style is called Lv (pronounced Looee) in Chinese. For this example, we take the following poem:

In Autumn, Evening Stays in the Mountains
Wang Wei

Kong shan xin yu hou
Tian qi wan lai qiu
Ming yue song jian zhao
Qing quan shi shang liu
Zhu xuan gui huan nv
Lian dong xia yu zhou
Sui yi chun fang xie
Wang sun zi ke liu

This specific poetic style is called Lv or Wu Lv in Chinese. That means 5-word (character), 8-line verse, as seen immediately above. The pattern of pronunciation (tongue) and rhyme is the same as in the "Deer Thicket" example, but the third and fourth or the fifth and sixth lines must match the alternating tongue. And the images of the third and fourth lines, or the fifth and six lines, should also use different poetic elements. Furthermore, they must match both sound and sense in two poetic lines called the antithesis. For example, in the poem "In Autumn, Evening Stays in the Mountain," the third line describes the bright moon (Ming yue), the fourth line uses the clear stream (Qing quan), the fifth line uses the bamboo noise (Zhu xuan), and the sixth line uses the lotus movement (Lian dong). This is a strict sequential variation of image types as well, and the even-number lines (2, 4, 6, 8 and sometimes 1) must rhyme – using in this case, the sound, "you," and must use contrasting metaphors in lines 2, 3, 4 and 6. Lines 3, 5, and 7 need not rhyme, and as for line 1, it may or may not rhyme with the even-numbered lines.

Besides Wu Jue or Wu Lv, there are other patterns: Qijue (4 lines of 7 characters), Qilv (8 lines of 8 characters), and Pailv (10 or more lines of 5 or 8 characters).

Now that we have briefly considered the ancient Chinese poetic style, we can contemplate using English to express this style. In my opinion, it's impossible – the two languages are totally different. As we know, different pronunciations of the same word express different meanings. For example, the Chinese word "Ma" has four tongues (pronunciations): the level tongue means "mother." The rising tongue means "numb," the departing tongue means "horse," and the entering tongue means "swear." So when I translate ancient Chinese poetry, though it's impossible to match the ancient Chinese poetic style, I submit such as the following:

Deer Thicket

Here on the mountain
No people can be seen,
But the sound of the voices
Of intruders you still perceive.
And here in the heart of the forest,
The glow of the setting sun
Is entering, and a shadow reflects upon
The carpet of green moss.

In Autumn, Evening Stays in the Mountains

After a fresh rain on the deserted mountain,
It's so cool, the gradual autumn evening.

Through the pine woods shines the moon;
Over the bare rock the rivulet is running.
Through the bamboo woods run whispers –
It's the washer-girls then going home.
The bobbing, dancing of the lotus flowers,
That is the fishing boats dragging nets.
I let go at last of the remembrance of spring loam –
I would like to enjoy, as do Wang Sun as they roam,
The wonder of the autumn sense.

The Tang Dynasty produced three very well-known poets: Li Bai, Du Fu, and Wang Wei. Among them, I very much prefer Wang Wei. His poetry always includes some Zen or Buddhist elements. I am a Buddhist and regularly meditate, and in following the writing in his poetry, I feel aligned with the period of the Tang Dynasty. His poetry is always full of Zen or Buddhism, and even painting or musical elements. Even a very short poem still shows this influence, as in:

The Valley of the Magnolia Flower
Wang Wei

The magnolia flower blooms in the treetops,
Its red face appearing high up in the mountains.
There are no people in the valley, and so
The flowers bloom, and fall one after another.

The Buddhist may say with deeper meaning: "The magnolia flowers always bloom and fall even though no one appreciates it." Human life is like a flower. I have imitated Wang Wei's poetry style in my own poetry:

Visit to the River Wang
David Du

Looking forward, no boat, no ferry appears there.
There's no grave yard, no village nearby.
Only the ginkgo tree stands there.
Only the tablet is breathing and

It is as if I see tears running from
The tree, tablet and river.

I wrote this poem last year when I visited Wang Wei's historic locale. Western people know Li Bai and Du Fu, but I believe they should also know Wang Wei. Specifically, they don't know the real meaning in Wang Wei's poetry. His poetry is very different from Li Bai's or Du Fu's. It's full of deeper meaning. Sometimes he even enters an animal's eyes to express the world, as in "Deer Thicket." He takes the deer's perspective to express that when danger is close to the vulnerable, the best plan is escape. But he uses a perceptive example to express the danger closing in—the glow of the setting sun never penetrates the heart of the forest unless someone (a hunter) is spreading the branches.

Although others have translated Wang Wei, when I read the original richness of his poetry, I am motivated to reintroduce him to the west in my own way.

This has been my dream. In particular, last year when I visited his old habitat, the Wang River area, there by the plaque in his remembrance, I saw only a solitary gingko tree. Nothing more. In China, Li Bai and Du Fu each have a museum remembering them. Only Wang Wei has become an unnoticed corner.

I feel I have a duty to try to reinterpret him. Not only did he write great classic poems, but also much Zen poetry. Poetry that is a light to illuminate the human road, a flower to bloom in the human heart.

David Du

CONTENTS

178. After Arriving at Huazhou I Watch Liyang Across the River and, Recall Ding San's Lodge
179. For Lay Buddhist Li at Xi River (On the Spot Where I Visit at Master Tan Bi's Temple)
180. A Gift Poem for My Sixth Uncle, Returning to Luhun
181. A Poem for Prefecture Chief Miao Fengqian at Jinyun
182. Hermit Li Lives on the Mountain
183. The Morning I Entered Xingyang City
184. Crossing the Yellow River to Qinghe
185. The Willow's Waves *(Wang River Collection)*
186. Pepper Plantation
187. Osprey Weir *(Poems at Huangpu Yue's Yunxi Villa)*
188. Shangping Field *(Poems at Huangpu Yue's Yunxi Villa)*
189. Duckweed *(Poems at Huangpu Yue's Yunxi Villa)*
190. I Heard Pei Di Made Poems – Then I Sent Him this Joyful Poem
191. The Portrait of Cui Xingzong.
192. Suspicious Dream
193. To Send Off Officer Li to Dongjiang
194. Sending Off Zhang Wu (Yin) to Xuancheng
195. Sending Off He Sui's Nephew
196. Sending Qiwu Qian Home After He Fails His State Examination
197. Hua Zi Gang *(Wang River Collection)*
198. Jinzhu Hill *(Wang River Collection)*
199. Sending Off Officer Yang to Guozhou
200. Dogwood

THE PULSE OF WANG WEI

1. Deer Thicket

Here on the barren mountain
No people can be seen,
But the sound of the voices
Of intruders you still perceive.

And here in the heart of the forest,
The glow of the setting sun
Is entering, and a shadow reflects upon
The carpet of green moss.

Deer Thicket: one of 20 famous sights built by Wang Wei near his villa during the Tang Dynasty.

The poem of Deer Thicket: Wang Wei built a feeding station for the wild deer, cared for them, and watched many of them get hunted down. The eyes noticing the normally shaded woods are the deer's. A wary deer will take alarm and flee to safety!

2. Songs in Wei City (Sending off Yuan Er to Anxi)

Moistening the soil in Wei City falls the dawn morning rain;
The willows seem extremely fresh on the hostel lawn.
O my old friend, you'd better drink one more glass of wine,
As there will be no old friend once you journey past Yangguan.

Anxi: refers to the Tang Dynasty protectorate set up by the Emperor to control the western regions, presently in Xinjiang Territory.

Wei City: refers to an old city in the Qin Dynasty, presently to the north-east of Xianyang City in Shaanxi Province.

Yangguan: located southwest of Dunhuang, about 70 miles from Dunhuang City. Built in the Han Dynasty era, it's a route to Xiyu (the Western Regions) in ancient China. Yangguan was a minor nation at the frontier.

3. The Gully of the Twittering Bird

When the people's voices end gradually,
The faint, recurring sounds of osmanthus
Blooms I hear, dropping throughout the gully…
At night now with the mountain
In spring so quiet and empty,
Even the moon seems aware of the bird
Whose song is twittering, intermittently.

This poem was written as a Title Poem for Wang Wei's friend Huangpu Yue, describing his Yunxi villa.

Title poem: a poetic style in ancient China used when someone wrote a poem to somebody according to a place, picture, or the thematic topic.

4. The Zhu Li Hostel

Sitting alone in a deeply quiet lea –
By a grove of bamboo –
Playing the lyre, then whistling loudly,
Here in the heart of the forest none know –
Only the moon comes with me!

Zhu Li Hostel: another one of 20 sights near Wang Wei's villa on the Wang River in Lantian County in Shaanxi Province in the Tang Dynasty.

5. A Visit to the Temple of Xiangji

I don't know where it is, the temple of Xiangji –
But after several miles climbing the mountain,
I see the summit, surrounded by clouds, above me.
The forest is too dense to find a road to begin
An approach that people can use. Among the trunks,
A bell sounds somewhere. The sound abides,
Of springs sobbing over their collapsed rocks.
The woods, so thick even the sunshine hides
In their shadows, make me feel the chill of a bad dream.
At twilight I hear the song coming from the empty stream.
I understand the sitting meditation that can start
To remove the evil dragon from the pool of my heart.

Temple of Xiangji: known presently as the temple of Fengxue or Qianfeng temple. It is located at the entrance of Mt. Fengxue, Ruzhou City in Henan Province.

evil dragon: Buddha's metaphor for the common people's illusion and evil thought.

6. In Autumn, Evening Stays in the Mountains

After fresh rain on the ethereal mountain,
It's so cool, the gradual autumn evening.
Through the pine woods shines the moon;
Over the bare rock the rivulet is running.
Through the bamboo woods run whispers –
It's the washer-girls then going home.
The bobbing, dancing of the lotus flowers,
That is the fishing boats dragging nets.
I let go at last of the fragrance of spring loam –
I would like to enjoy, as do Wang Sun as they roam,
The wonder of the autumn sense.

Wang Sun: hermit or traveler.

7. Missing My Brother Who Lives at Shan Dong (Sept 9th)

I'm living in a strange place as a stranger,
And furthermore, I miss you, my brother.
When here I run into the 9/9 festival on this day,
I imagine you on the mountain down your way.
When you will smell the dogwood blossom
You're wearing then, you will miss one person.
(Me.)

Shan Dong: refers to the east of Mt. Huashan, Wang Wei's hometown (Yongji county in Shanxi Province) is located in the east of Mt. Huashan.

Dogwood: represents brother.

9/9 festival: a September festival of seniors during which people always climb the mountain and wear crowns of dogwood flowers.

8. To a Maiden (Mo Chou) in Luoyang

There's a maid in Luoyang, who lived opposite my door.
She was very beautiful, though only fifteen, immature.
During her wedding time, the bridegroom rode a Cong horse
That came from Yu Le, and maidservants presented the main course,
A gold tray with cooked carp, an impressive dish, to be sure.
In her bridegroom's home, the pavilion of painted pictures,
A red high building with terraces and open halls–were all
Opposite each other. Red peach flowers, green willows
Grow on all the filamented eaves, shake with the billows
Of the wind with the silk curtains hanging on the wall.
She has sent for the scented cart made with metal shoes
For the perfect fans she has sent to the splendid bedroom.
Young and extremely frivolous, but rich, is the groom.
His extravagance stands out like rich man Ji lun's, whose
Spendthrift ways were famous back in the Jin Dynasty.
He loves his bride, teaching her song and dances of gaiety,
And not even caring to send coral jewelry to the others.
They enjoyed their lives overnight, not like sisters/brothers –
The candlelight came out through the window until daybreak.
Snuff drifts along the patterned window lattices in a slow take…
After they both have fun, she never reviews the melody,
Merely makes up and sits with an incense burner, carelessly.
In Luoyang City I knew people with all richness and luxury,
People who come and go, influential families like Zhao or Li.
In the Han era, who cared if pretty-girl Xi Shi lives her dream –
When she was poor, she only washed silk dresses at Ruoye stream.

Cong horse: a good quality horse with a bluish-white mane. Its native land is Xin Jiang territory; only rich people can afford them.

Yu Le: Jade bridle.

Ji Lun: a very rich man in the Jin Dynasty. His other name is Shi Chong.

coral jewelry: an idiom, from Shi Chong: once upon a time, Wang Kai, a senior officer took a two-foot branch of coral, a gift from the Emperor, to send to Shi Chong. Shi used a hammer to break it up, and when Shi heard Wang was very angry, Shi asked his subordinates to send Wang a four-foot coral tree!

Zhao: refers to Zhao Feiyan, a Queen of Cheng in Han Dynasty. She used her beauty to gain the King's love, and Emperor Cheng spoils her for 20 years. She and her family became a rich household, rising from common status.

Li: Li Ping the Emperor's concubine; she also became a rich person due to the Emperor's spoils.

Xi Shi: she is one of "the four ancient beauties," a beautiful woman in Yue State in the Spring and Autumn and the Warring States periods. She used the honey trap on Wu's King to help Yue State wipe out Wu State. But before she went to the Wu Palace, she was a washer girl and washed clothing at Ruo Ye Stream.

Ruoye Stream: a stream at Xi Shi's hometown Zhuji, a city in Zhejiang Province. Xi Shi washed clothes there.

9. A Poem for Mr. Zhang Shaofu

In the setting sun I prefer quiet, unconcern
About anything in the world. There's no turn
Of thoughts about what can benefit the country,
So I live in solitude, secluded as I might be,
In the deep and quiet woods. The wind may choose
To sigh through the pines and blow my belt loose.
The moon shines over the mountain and I enjoy my lyre.
My advice on becoming an officer, or not? You inquire…
I do not directly answer, but please listen to the fisherman's song
Coming over the lake's deep weeds the bayshore curves along.

Fisherman's song: a hermit song.

10. A Sendoff on the Mountain

After we say goodbye to each other on the mountain,
I slowly close and latch this old wooden door of mine.
Year by year, in spring the grasses always get new green;
However, as a traveler, I don't know whether you'll return.

11. Gossip

You come from my home town,
You should know the latest from
My hometown. When you come
Back to meet me, let it be known
To me whether the plum tree down
By my patterned window is in blossom?

patterned window: carved or patterned window in ancient Chinese house.

12. Spring Water

When walking alone at the location
Named *Yellow Flower* – a river,
I always see spring water there.
The springs zigzag around the mountain,
For a distance of over a hundred miles,
Their sounds, their voices roaring
And their momentum ripping
But their colours remaining tranquil
As the pine woods around the spring.
I can enjoy the sparkly water chestnut,
The reeds reflecting like gold, or brighter.
That keeps my heart quiet and shut;
That is very similar to spring water,
Please come to the Yellow Flower –
Let's go fishing right now! Sure!

Yellow Flower: a river also called the Huanghua River located near Huanghua Town in the northeast of Feng County in Shaanxi Province.

13. Boating on the Han River

The Han River locates the name of Chu,
And joins the regions of Xiang, well, three.
And it links nine tributaries of the Yangtze
Over in Jiangmen County, quite a few.
Its mighty body runs outside the boundary.
Its colour makes the mountains appear or disappear,
And floating on its surface the castles that are near.
Its waves flow like the sky moving on,
A very splendid view in Xiangyang…
Let's become drunk with Mr. Shan Jian!

Han River: the largest tributary of the Yangtze River, it contains nine other tributaries and crosses Shaanxi and Hubei Provinces and the three Xiang Counties of Hunan Province (Xiaoxiang, Lixiang and Zhengxiang).

Three regions of Xiang: please see the footnote about Han River.

Jiangmen County: A Hubei Province location.

Chu: Chu State existed in the Spring and Autumn and Warring States periods; the majority of its land is contained currently in Hunan and Hubei Provinces. The first poet Mr. Qu Yuan, was born in Chu.

Xiangyang: a place in Hubei Province.

Shan Jian: the son of Shan Tao, one of the seven sages of the Bamboo Grove. Shan Jian liked drink; though he became an officer and enjoyed the leisurely lifestyle, and always drank too much, he was incorruptible in office(!).

14. Acacia

In the south of the country, red beans thrive.
In spring are they popping up, with a drive,
Blooming some new branch of vivaciousness.
On your trip there, I hope you'll pick up a mess.
They are the best ones for heart sickness.

red beans: also called the "yearning of love beans," a plant that grows in the south of Five Mountains in southern China (presently Guangdong Province and Hong Kong Territory). The beans are red, their shape very similar to peas. Once upon a time in Ancient China, a couple had a very deep love, but the husband went on a trip and contracted a serious illness and died. His wife was waiting for him, but he never came back. His wife was very sad and cried every day. Finally, she died by a tree close by her house. Then by the tree grew up plants that produced the red beans that people all said were dyed by the lady's blood. Now it has become a symbol for the yearning of love, always used by the poets.

15. The Isolation of Mount Song

Clear water runs both through and along
The vast woods and by the mountain road,
Circling, isolating, towering Mount Song.
I ride along leisurely on the horse cart load.
The fast-running water sounds as if it would
Like to come along with me; from the woods
The flock of dust-birds escorts me, lively.
The ruined castle waits close by the old ferry,
The setting sun lights the autumn mountain.
I settle down here from far away, to begin
Secluding, locking myself away in isolation.

16. An Emissary Visits the Frontier

With a few parcels from home, and a scant retinue,
I'm in a horse cart off to the frontier, to support and renew
The troops. On the way, as a Dian Shu Guo officer,
An emissary, I'm visiting Juyan. I feel like the poor
Traveling grasses invading, growing over
Ancient fortresses from the Han Dynasty, or
A goose flying back to the struggle in the North.
Here the beacon's one thin smoke shows its worth,
Rising straight up in the large desert, just over
From the falling sun set round in the huge river.
I meet the patrol officer when I arrive at Xiaoguan,
Who tells me where the commander is: at Yanran –
The frontline.

Dian Shu Guo: a "formalities" official who received the emissaries who visited the capital Chang An from abroad.

An emissary: Although Wang Wei writes in the first person singular, he does not indicate himself but takes the voice of an indeterminate emissary. This emissary hopes to be greeted by the commander, but it seems the commander is avoiding him. On the other hand, the frontline action is urgent, perhaps?

Juyan: a place located in the northern part of E Er Ji Na area of Inner Mongolia, a very important military town in ancient China.

the beacon's one thin smoke: when scouts see peace in the country, this is their signal.

Xiaoguan: a place located in the south east of Guyuan County in Ningxia Territory, also a very important military town in ancient China.

Yanran: the original meaning refers to a mountain in Mongolia, which later became a metaphor for the front line of the border.

17. On the Mountain

Less Jingxi water races past bare white rocks where
It's so cold that few maples shine their colours there.
The dry paths of the mountains no rain relieves
But the dark green jungle's endless tangled leaves,
Moistened with the dew, still wet my sleeves.

Jingxi (Jing Stream): a stream located at Mt. Qinling of Lantian County in Shaanxi Province.

18. The Valley of the Magnolia Flowers

A magnolia flower blooms in a treetop bower,
Its red face appearing high up in the mountains.
There's no people in the valley, it re-begins:
The flowers bloom and fall one after another.

The valley of the magnolia flower: the one of 20 sights nearby the Wang Wei's villa in Wang River Lantian County in Shaanxi Province in Tang Dynasty.

19. The Village by the Wei River

The setting sun shines through the village,
Cattle plodding home along the deep lane.
Worried about his grandson away all day
In the fields, an elder waits, despite his age,
As if stuck by his door. The turkeys crow
And the wheat's new heads nod to agree.
Silkworms are going to sleep about now,
Mulberry's leaves seem to grow sparsely,
Say the farmers, shouldering their hoes,
Laughing, talking – it's hard to say goodbye.
How I admire carefree scenes like those!
I can't help chanting emotionally – no lie –
The Book of Song.

The Book of Song: the earliest poetry book in China, written in the Zhou Dynasty before the Spring and Autumn period. It is an anthology of early poems collected by the State Poetry Collecting Officer. Its characteristic is that the poems are all written with four characters in each line. In later ages, almost all poets learn from this book.

20. Mengcheng Ao

Settling down in a new home at Meng Cheng Kou,
I see a little old tree, the remains of a withered willow.
After I have left, this home will be owned by who?
No use being sad for the old owner's goods, though –

Mengcheng Ao (Meng Cheng Kou): located by a gate of the Wang River, another of the 20 sights near Wang Wei's villa on the Wang River in Lantian County in Shaanxi Province during the Tang Dynasty.

21. Luanjia Lai

The rustling, heavy, autumn rains,
Rushing, running on the stoney rock,
Splash the egret's body – it exclaims!
Then up it flies, reacting to its shock.
But after looking around from up high
And seeing it was only water raging by,
It returns peacefully.

Luanjia Lai: located at an entrance of the Wang River, one of 20 sights.

22. The Lacquer Tree in the Garden (The Qiyuan)

He does not brag, the ancient person, Zhuangzi…
As he recalls lacking the ability to manage the state.
He is serving as a minor officer now, occasionally,
With only a few struggling trees left in the open-late
Government garden he manages to manage, patiently.

Zhuangzi: a very famous sage in the Warring States Period. He was born in Song Country and followed Laozi who created Taoism. He emphasized that all things can be used but they do not belong to anyone. He used to be an officer at Qiyuan, a lacquer tree garden in the Royal Yard. He is a famous philosopher, ideologist, litterateur, and his essays have become examples many writers study.

23. After the Rain, I'm Watching the Freshness

After the rain, I'm watching the fresh wilderness –
I see no dust or fog; it's very vast and bare and clean.
The gate of the castle is close to the ferry address,
The foliage by the village hides the mouth of the stream.
The fast-running water's out-ridges shine and glisten,
And green summits jump up from the mountain's chine.
Now it's time for farming work – I can't see any men
Of leisure. Busy in the fields, all families stay aligned.

24. A Poem in the Rain at Wang River Villa

It has been rainy for days… the woods seem empty, quiet,
And the cooking smoke rises less and less straightly.
Villagers steam the goosefoot vegetable, boil glutinous millet.
These they'll carry the mile to the field where they
Can find their relatives farming. I can see the egrets flying
Over the wild paddy fields in summer, and orioles are singing
Among the dense shadows. I have the habit of watching
The hibiscus in the mountain bud or bloom or fall,
And of picking up okra under the pines; I don't encroach.
I have no wish to jostle for a seat with others, not at all.
Why do they, like wild seagulls, still doubt my approach?

Wang River (also called Wangchuan): Wang Wei built a villa on this river, which existed in his Tang Dynasty era, now rather difficult to find, but presently around the location of Wangchuan town, Lantian county, Shaanxi Province. It is about 60 kms from Chang An (now Xi'an).

Jostling for a seat: the idiom comes from the book, "Zhuangzi." It tells of Mr. Yang Zhu (a philosopher who lived in the Warring States period) who followed Laozi on the road, to learn Taoism. The first time he stayed in a hostel where the owner and the tenants were jostling for every seat, he was granted a seat reserved for him. But when he did further studies with Laozi and came back to stay at this hostel again, nobody yielded their seat for him. This indicates somebody had learned a natural, harmonious way to fit in with the people.

Wild seagulls: this idiom comes from the book, *Liezi.* It tells of a boy who established a good relationship with wild seagulls. The seagulls always came very close to him. The boy's father heard this news and asked his son to trap and capture the seagulls. However, the seagulls no longer would approach him!

25. Chaotic Moment in the Mountains

I'm living lonely, I close the door, and the sun
I watch going down, shining on the mountain.
Returning to their nests up in the pines, the cranes
Arrive. Few visitors come to my poor house.
The baby bamboo grows new shoots from canes;
The red lotus lets fall its old petals by a mouse.
At the ferry the cooking smoke is rising;
I can see the people who've been gathering
Water chestnuts now everywhere returning.

26. The Old General

When I was fifteen, twenty years old, I'd seize
Bare handed the enemy's horses on the go.
I was young and strong, killing those enemies,
Those fearless, lethal, fierce tigers – heroic, no?
Like Huang Xuer of Yexia, yes?
I have had uncountable battles,
Swinging my sword against many foes, sure,
Our troops like explosions of falcons, when
Enemy horses, in fear, rode into each other.
Our General Wei Qing was helped by Heaven,
And Heaven is never defeated. Just the same,
Li Guang, though on our side, played the card
Wild Goose Chasing – bad luck's his middle name –
And in the end missed every royal reward.

Since I have retired, my physique has declined,
As for it, and world affairs, time is always changing, and so fast.
Now my hair is getting grey and my face is lined.
Due to lack of exercise, my old Hou Yi bow arm loses power at
last…
Nowadays my left elbow pains – a bone spur.
I sell melons by the public roads like an impoverished, wandering
Aristocrat, and plant willows by my door
And follow routine days, unfazed, like venerable Tao Yuanming.
Old trees in the cold, sparse in the deep lane, make a silent team,
And my lonely windows face a scattering of deserted mountains.
Learning, like Geng Gong at Chi Le, to dig a well and find a stream,
I never complain like the old drunks seated at Yingchuan's.

The battle clouds begin to gather under Mount He Lan;
Emergency letters from the front are sent out day and night.
Special envoys at San He recruit every strong young man.
Five times recently, an imperial edict asks me to the fight,
To become a general again. Snow starts to glitter
Just like shining armour, and I look over my war sword,
My eyes tracing its seven-star pattern – I remember.
I dream of a good Yan Country-quality bow, and more:

I dream of I myself killing the enemy's commander.
I won't let any foreign troops offend our King.
Don't say the old general at Yun Zhong is cashing in
On his former position – the enemy I can still defeat with honour.

Note that Wang Wei does not write about himself in this poem, and for that matter, often uses the first person simply to express the point of view of the person in his poem.

Huang Xuer of Yexia: Huang Xuer was born in the Three Kingdoms Period, the son of Cao Cao, who was a prime minister in the Country of Wei. He had a yellow beard and used to go to war and fight very bravely. A rank of nobility was conferred upon him at Yexia, in Linzhang County in Hebei Province.

Wei Qing: used to be an equerry following the Princess of Ping Yang. Then he married her and became a Han Dynasty General Commander and mustered the troops to fight the Sino-barbarians. Due to these contributions, the title of Marquis was conferred upon him.

Li Guang: He came from a family of generals and, as one of the Seven Prefectures, he participated in battles to fight the Sino-barbarians over 100 times and killed uncountable enemies. He gained a famous name: The Tiger General. But unfortunately, he didn't receive the title of Marquis. When he was responsible for delaying the fulfillment of a subsequent military plan, he committed suicide.

Hou Yi: It is said he was born in the ancient time of The Sovereign and Five Emperors and had high skill in archery: the legend is that there used to be 10 suns in the sky and the world was much too hot. Hou Yi used his skill to shoot out 9 of the suns. His wife was Chang E who stole and ate a magic elixir and left her husband to go to The Moon Palace.

Geng Gong: A General in the Han Dynasty. Once he was in Chi Le, an area bordering the Sino-barbarians. The Sino-barbarian troops encircled Chi Le and cut the source of water, but Geng Gong dug a well in the castle and survived.

old drunks at Yingchuan's: an idiom that comes from Mr. Guan Fu, quite the personality, who always curried favour with the rich and powerful, even abusing officers when roaring drunk. He was very rich in complaint when drunk and finally the Emperor accepted minister Tian Fen's suggestion to put him death.

Mt. He Lan: a mountain between Ningxia Territory and Inner Mongolia. And a border area between the Han Nation and the Sino-barbarians.

old general at Yunzhong: an idiom that comes from a famous Prefect, Wei Shang, in the Han Dynasty Poems. He managed his troops according to military discipline, cared for his soldiers well, gave them preferential treatment, and killed uncountable enemies. Yunzhong is located presently in the northeast of Tuo ke tuo in Inner Mongolia.

27. The Temple of Shimen Jingshe on Mount Lantian

The landscape of mountain and spring
Is so beautiful at the hour of the setting sun.
Driving the boat, with the wind blowing,
I feel very satisfied. Enjoying every one
Of the wonders, I don't feel I've travelled so far.
Though I drove past the fountainhead unawares,
I am excited to see the woods around the temple far away,
As at the beginning I doubted I was driving the right way.
However, amazingly, the river turned around, began flowing
Again toward the front of the looming Mountain.
I moor the boat and take a relaxing walk with a cane –
Exactly the place that I want to be – it's so satisfying.
Under pine shadows, a few elderly monks take rest.
They are so relaxed. Before dawn, monks are busying
Themselves for their morning classes and tests.
In the evening time they're doing Zen,
And it seems quieter on the mountain.
Ask the cowherd about the core of Taoism, his belief;
Inquire of the woodcutter about the affairs of human life.
I stay there napping by the forests or sleeping in bed
With the incense smoking. I can enjoy the wild fragrance
Filling my robes from the mountain valley, instead.
The moon jumped from the summit and ever since
It's reflecting on the hanging cliff…I want to further
Explore but I worry about losing my way even more,
So I can only await the daybreak to be climbing soon.
With a smile I appreciate people who're living there,
Like those living in the Fairyland of Peach Bloom.
I expect to return when red flowers all the trees will bear.

Mt. Lantian: a mountain close to the Wang River in Shaanxi Province.

28. A Poem at the Spring Garden

Turtledoves are twittering
On the roof – it's spring;
This side of the village,
The apricot flowers bring
On the blossoms stage
So much, it seems a rage
Of white. The many farmers
Are getting busy on their chores:

Some of them trimming the mulberry,
Others shouldering their hoes to go
Look for the fountainhead, where it can be.
The swallow comes back – it will know
Its old nest from the time one year ago.
The household is checking the new calendar.
I use a Shang to pour my drink but suddenly I stop, remember…

The man who left here before, and can't
Enjoy this scenery. I feel despondent.

Shang: a utensil to drink or pour wine, like the wine cup of ancient China.

29. Watching Some Hunting

With strong bow shots despite the rough spring winds,
The General is hunting out in the Wei City suburbs,
His eagle eyes getting quicker as withered grass begins,
The horseshoes racing lighter as melted snow curbs.
In a few minutes he has passed by Xin-Feng Town
And returned to where the military is camped down.
Look back at the place where he was hunting the fen –
The distant clouds are so wide and flat toward heaven.

Wei City: a place located to the northwest of Xi'an, Shaanxi Province.

Xin-Feng Town: a town close to Xi'an in Shaanxi Province, in Ancient China. It's very famous for its Wine Market.

Xi Liu: a place located in the Chang An district in Shaanxi Province. In the Han Dynasty it was very famous as a military camp managed by General Zhou Yafu.

30. At Parting

I am asking you to dismount and tie your horse;
I offer you a drink, and a friendly ear, of course.
I ask where you're going, where you've been sent;
You say your official life is a living discontent.
You wish that you could find some seclusion
In the forested foothills of Mount Zhongnan…
You can go do as you do like, my friend.
I don't ask you for your reason. Without end
Are the white clouds, there upon the mountain.

Mount Zhongnan: a famous mountain where hermits lived, close to the Middle of Qin Ling. The entire area extended from Wu Gong Country to Lantian Country in Shanxi Province. This mountain was inhabited by a combination of Taoists, Buddhists, and hermits. In Ancient China, many hermits lived there to do their meditation. Wang Wei also lived here for over ten years. Its other name is Nan-Shan.

31. The Fairyland of Peach Blossoms

Through beautiful spring, the fishing boat floats downstream,
Peach blossoms blooming on both banks of the old river.
Watching red trees passing by, losing track of near or far,
Approaching the stream's end, the fisherman, as if in a dream,
Might be seeing a distant settlement indistinctly… he's pitched
Down a deep and obscure mountain cataract; suddenly there
Is open land, cloudy sky upon which tiny green trees are stitched.

Floating into a village, he watches long bamboo fences appear,
Strewn with flowers door to door all along the river scene.
He meets a villager, who claims he never did the name *Han* hear.
The inhabitants all wear antique clothing in the style of Qin.
Generations must have lived here beside the Wu Ling River (his guess)
From so long ago – and have built a fairyland out of their remoteness.

When it's night the moon shines down upon it
And the houses in the pines seem oh so quiet,
Yet in the rising sun cocks crow, dogs bark their best.
Surprised to see him, villagers greet him as their guest,
And graciously invite him to their homes, and
Ask him questions about the outer homeland.
In the early morning, every household sweeps a load
Of delicate flower petals from their portions of the road.
At dusk, fishermen and foresters come back home by boat.

They said long ago ancestors fled the disastrous world hell
When they found this land of peach blossoms, hidden well.
None knew that a people could be established there in solitude;
From outside it seems a desert mountain where clouds brood.
The fisherman sees the rarity of this uncovered treasure,
And though he wants to live there, he can't, he's sure,
Abandon thinking of his former world with pleasure…

Only when he gets back home, he can't forget the fairyland.
And so he makes plans for a return – he'd visited before, and

In spite of mountains and water hazards, hunger and isolation,
He bravely tells himself he cannot fail to reach his destination.
But inexplicably, the mountain valleys have completely changed.
He remembers how the river deepened toward the mountain range
And how, zigzagging down the stream, currents pulled him, lost,
To the hidden world and friendly people who had been his host.

At last, the more he looks, the more it seems he's blind.
Although the fallen blossoms float everywhere he can see,
He starts to realize he never will retrace his journey or refind
The way to the hidden paradise or know where it might be.

Han: (First, 25-220 BC; Second, 208-2 BC.) The Second Feudal Dynasty was built by Liu Bang, due to Wang Mang usurping power and establishing the New Dynasty. Han is divided into two periods: West Han and East Han. After the Old Hua Xia Nation (Huaxia), the Han Nation started to support a nobility. In the Han Dynasty, Korea and Vietnam belonged to China.

Wu Ling Yuan (Wu Ling Hill): it is also called a fairy land of peach flowers: said to be a fairyland on earth. It is in Changde County in Hunan Province.

Qin (pronounced Cheen): The first Feudal Dynasty was built by the First Emperor Ying Zheng (221 BC). As well, it's the first Unified dynasty. Qin destroyed six other states: Han, Zhao, Wei, Chu, Yan, Qi, but unified them into a great country – China.

32. A Bit of Gossip

The parents, who are like a couple of swallows,
Begin to instruct their daughter, who follows,
A peach flower only newly bloomed, so soft.
Handsome boys Like Wang Chang to the east
Live very nearby, and Song Yu to the west.
She is very young, but she can weave silk cloth,
And goes to the river to wash her silk dresses.
Her behaviour attracts a proper man who addresses
Her…and soon his wedding cart of scented wood
Is stopping by her small house of Nan Mo. Good.

Wang Chang: a handsome man who lived in the Wei and the Jin Dynasties. When he would go out on tour, so many girls would notice and admire him.

Song Yu: a handsome man who was born in Song Country in the Warring States Period. He was known as one of the ten most handsome men. He also had a great skill in writing ancient essays. He moved from Song to Chu and became a special attendant to the King of Chu. In Chu his essays are famous, like another poet, Qu Yuan. His most representative work is *To the Wind.*

Nan Mo: a farming family

33. More Gossip

In the morning when I pick up a willow branch,
I meet you in a corner of Luoyang – by chance?
I have a husband as did pretty Qin Luofu;
I don't want to be a concubine like Chu.
My husband and I drink wine in jade goblets,
In warm candlelight, I take off my cotton jacket.
If you meet a man on a horse – do you understand –
Leading thousands of people, that is my husband.
He is a great man. Please inform Jin Wu Zi, your master:
Take your betrothal gifts like the jade pot, and scatter!

Qin Luofu: a pretty girl who lived in Han Dan City in the East Han Dynasty. She is known as The Mulberry Woman in Chinese literature. She married the handsome man Wang Ren, who worked for the Emperor's Uncle (Royal Highness Zhao). One Day Zhao went out on a tour to the suburbs and noticed Qin Luo Fu among those picking mulberries. He was infatuated by her beauty, but fearing for his reputation of incorruptibility, couldn't grab her, so he asked a matchmaker to come to talk to her. She refused his advances and in response, played a now-famous song in China, "A Song of Luofu."

Jin Wu Zi: a senior official position, a supervisor of the Royal Troops guarding the capital and its people.

34. About Xi Shi

As the world always admires, a lot,
The beauty of the young feminine,
A most beautiful girl (Xi Shi) could not
For long stay poor and unknown.

Originally she was a mere wash-girl
At the Ruo Ye stream in Yue place;
Of late she becomes an Imperial
Concubine in a Wu national palace.

Did you think she had something plus,
Different from others, when she was poor?
After she received her regal status,
Everybody recognized her rare allure.

Who now puts her make up on? Many maids of honour!
And never does she need to dress her lovely self.
Since the king's been spoiling her, she looks more tender.
Charmed, he never ever pays attention to her faults.

The girl who washed dresses with her at her start,
In the old days at the stream of Ruoye,
Now no longer gets to ride in the same cart.
I should inform this neighbour, Dong Shi,
That it's very hard to get love a king allows
If all you know is how to frown your brows.

Dong Shi: a neighbour of Xi Shi, an ugly girl who heard from everyone about Xi Shi being very beautiful. Xi Shi sometimes became ill and would then frown her brows. So Dong Shi learnt to frown her brows that way, but no one thought Dong Shi was beautiful. People laughed at her. Later this story became an idiom for people who want to imitate someone but instead end by making their status worse than before.

35. A Hint of Gossip

I live in propinquity with the Mengjin River,
And the Mengjin ferry is opposite my door.
There's often moored some boat that's from around
My hometown – southern China, some way down.
Are there also any letters from my hometown?

36. Further Gossip

I have seen the plum trees blooming
And I’ve heard the bluebird twittering –
Yet, my heart is spring grass shoots
That fear growing where fall boots.

37. For the Young Soldiers

(1)
Xinfeng produces the good quality wine, although it's pricey.
As well, Xianyang City gathers errant heroes, some only cubs.
To friends, and meeting to drink together there, they are all loyalty.
They are all hitching their horses on the willow tree by the pub.

(2)
He was an officer guarding the Emperor's own safety,
But he resigned to follow the General in charge
Of the army joining battle and attacking Yuyang City.
He understood the border is very hard to guard.
However, for his service the state easily sacrificed his bright life.
People still sense a fragrance in his bones. The flesh was brief.

(3)
He could draw the bow on his left or on his right,
Even as being encircled by many enemy warriors.
He thought it nothing threatening, that deadly fight –
He reclined on his gold saddle, and aimed his arrows,
Killing many enemy commanders, one after another.

(4)
The Emperor and Generals end the banquet with winks and nudges,
The Generals discussing their battle achievements all the whiles.
The Emperor comes and awards everyone with properties, badges.
The Generals wear rewards, leave Mingguang Palace with smiles.

(1) *Xianyang:* a capital of the Qin Dynasty; many chivalrous persons lived there. In this poem, Wang Wei refers to his capital, Chang An.

(2)Yuyang:ancient place presently Qi county Tianjin city.

(4) Mingguang Palace: a palace where the Emperor made banquets or celebrated victories or sent off Generals.

38. A Moment's Feeling

After the drizzle, the sky is solid grey, unmarred.
Even in the daytime I would rather shut the door,
And sit to watch the green mass of my courtyard,
Its colours seemingly, virtually, dying the robe I wear.

39. A Poem for the Frontier

The rebels hunted out of lawless Ju Yan City, to glide
Behind the burning grass, hunting with smoke and fire,
Hiding the dust from their horses as they onward ride
Across the wild autumnal plain, behind where fire flickers –
The best place for hunting vultures, the skeleton-pickers.

In the morning our soldiers are guarding our fortification, then
At night our general attacks the enemy's armed encampment.
Finally, our troops get the victory over the horde,
And I will come by, representing the Emperor.
I will give to the great General Cui Xiyi
Who's like Huo Qubing in the Han Dynasty,
Many gifts such as a sword with a jade handle upon it,
A rhinoceros horn bow, and a fine horse with a jade bit.

Cui Xiyi: a Deputy General Commander at Anxi who put down a revolt from the Tupo Nation in Qinghai Province.

Huo Qubing: Wei Qing's nephew, a very famous General in the West Han Dynasty. He directed 6 attacks against the (Sino-) barbarians and all of them were great victories, for which he received many distinguished awards, and a company of Hussars (Biao Ji or Biao Yao was their General). Unfortunately, he passed away too young – only 23 years old. His cause of death remains unknown.

40. A Poem for Officer Guo

The setting sun is bathing the high villa's pavilion
And the courtyard of your house, overlooking
The flowers of the peach and plum trees, whereon
The fluff of nearby willow trees keeps flying.
There, many committed disciples follow you.
You work very hard, even as the evening bell,
Less often in the officials' houses, rings through.
And then you go to bed in a dream, sleep well.
In the morning you hear only the bird twittering
Its quite lawless suit. You wear the robe tinkling
With jade decorations to go to meet the Emperor at the palace,
And by the day's end you hold an imperial edict in both hands.
At the closing of the complex evening court, I want to trace
And to follow your comings and goings and all your plans.
But it's hopeless – getting always older and ever sicker,
Ill in bed, I must often miss meetings with the Emperor.

Officer Guo: a friend of Wang Wei's, holding the official positions of palace steward, supervising secretary, and censor.

41. Two Poems for People Learning About Buddhism
(When Lay Buddhist Hu and I Both Fall Ill)

(1)
Once, as sudden as a carnal thought rising,
Yes, you were born like the dew in the morning –
If you see the after world like this, how can you
Concern yourself about people's who's who?

Of course, the way of mastery is to minimize possession
But inclining toward emptiness doesn't equal subordination.
Don't you know that washing the evil, conniving heart
Can free you from the Samsara, give you a new start?
I think if enlightenment, the way of Buddha, lifts
You out of the line of the lost, it's one of his gifts –
Desire's potent seed occasions sickness, you see,
Yet you follow the greedy, start to realize poverty.
Ah, but colour and songs are not themselves a big deal…
Temporary appearances…am I myself more real?
How is the way of Buddha set up? What do you think of
His various paths for the heart, for sweeping the dirt off?
Of course, you, Mr. Hu, can rest easy but who
Can follow your aloneness, learning through
The way of Buddhism? Who overcomes their desire
For wealth, and goes for understanding, to inquire
About the way of Buddha, and who would rather spend
A secluded life, a life that could connect to that without end?

Did they know what the nature of change or decay meant?
So – how could they talk about intimacy and estrangement?

(2)
If you think the way of Buddha is empty,
You only fade away on an endless way.
If you think it is real, you must really
Go along with it in a way that's leisurely.

Get in one of buddha's vehicles – but which vehicle is best?
The one you ride on, already behind you, on which you rest.

You keep yourself without serious ambition
And alive without care about illness or nutrition,
Or even poverty and you don't care about the ring
Of birth and death – you don't worry about anything.

You take a horse as your example, as a bodhisattva does,
You even liken yourself to a placid cow, like Lao-tzu does.
Plant happiness in a temple like Master Jia Ye does –
Devote benevolence and laugh just like Confucius.

Any river can carry our boats, any road can bear our carts:
If you concentrate on that and think about that in your heart,
You, Mr. Hu, will take a wrong way. All things gathering
Are like all empty flowers, scattering and dispersing.
The emptiness is the flower fading, then later, blooming.
The worry is a tree budding then after, losing its leaves.
If you put away any thought of appearance or grooming,
You'll be glad to be an unremembered person no one grieves.
If you have desire in your heart, even if you do sitting meditation,
You still have some inherent needs that you must patiently shun.

Like Huang Quan did: he capitulated in the Country of Wu
And then forgot himself over again in the Country of Shu.

If I have said something unsatisfactory to you,
Please do not consider that I wish to bother you.

Jia Ye: he's called Maha Kassapa or Mo He Jia Ye after a very Buddhist-famous disciple of Shakyamuni, one of 10. His greatest personality trait was having no obsessions. The famous story that shows his feature: one day Shakyamuni picked up a flower and showed it to all his disciples. Only Mo He Jia Ye said nothing with a smile, like Buddha did. After Shakyamuni passed away, Mo He Jia Ye gathered the first meeting to collect the teachings of Buddha. He became the foremost leader in spreading Buddhism. Zen Buddhism respects him as the first Master of Zen.

Huang Quan: A General in Shu Country in the Three kingdoms period. In the beginning he was a military officer with Liu Zhang then Liu Zhang was beaten by Liu Bei. He capitulated to Liu Bei, then followed Liu to attack Wu Country. After losing this battle, he capitulated to Wei Country, but…still became a senior officer and spent a life of wealth.

42. The Zen Master at Yan Zi Kan

There's a temple in the mountain, its name is Yan Zi Kan. I trust
When you visit you'll see how narrow the path is, how precipitous –
When the surface of the road is cracked, it's serious for all of us.

In contrast, how simply, straight and steep, the summit reaches sky.
With a musical sound, waterfalls and streams descend from on high.
The threatening, monstrous rock seems about to fall to destruction.
Nothing controls such floods – not the famous engineer Bo Yu –
Though Five Titans watch, they fear to begin dam construction!
However, a great master – to himself remaining traditionally true –
Doesn't involve himself in mundane details, but brings to bear
His meditation: the pavilions fill in, in the auspicious air there.

Morning to midnight (six times a day) he sounds the bronze gong,
Gathering the disciples. He eats only 1 meal as the day goes along –
His belts plunge into his waist. Under brilliant white clouds shining,
They're cultivating land and cutting lacquer trees, sound rebounding
Through the red valley. When he goes out, only the ape, picking up
Chestnuts, follows behind. When he returns, with his empty cup,
He's only accompanied by the crane that nests on the pine tree's
top.
Sometimes he prays to the god of mountains, and does not stop –
Occasionally meeting the immortal who lives in the cave,
Who comes to entrust him with his divine messages to save,
Using merciful compassion, lost human souls on the fence.
Let humans see: the heart is Buddha; give up persistence.

I tire of scenic spots and historic resorts like nearby ancient Zhou.
Instead I would rather enjoy the Shu Place scenery, Yan Zi Kan,
too.
Look, the cave opens at the centre of the mountain rock so wide,
The external gully is completely tumbled down on both sides.
The temple bridge is built by wood brought down by the breeze.
The gate's bars are tied tight by rattan vines dropped by the trees.

Even birds don't fly there. The cave is getting dried up.
Who can cross the running river with clothes tucked up?

It's impossible to climb by hand the steep cliff, it's a fright!
There the woods are so thick; the middays are but twilight.
At that time the master returned to sitting meditation, brave,
Intently cultivating his Buddha self at his temple in the cave,
No matter how excessive the growth that spring grasses gave.

Bo Yu: he is also called Yu, a descendent of the Yellow Emperor; he made the very great contribution of preventing floods by water control. He instituted the important *Ding* ritual bronze cauldrons representing the Hua Xia Nation (Nine regions). It is said he established the first Country (Dynasty) – Xia.

Five titans: it is said the famous Five Titans in Old Shu Nation had marvellous energy and guarded the Old Shu nation. The King of Qin wanted to wipe out the Old Shu nation; he brewed a plot: he asked his workers to make five bulls and put some gold under the bulls in the shape of excrement, then set them up among the Qin and Old Shu. Then he sent a message to the King of Old Shu. The King of Old Shu was very greedy; he asked the Five Titans to carry the golden bulls back to Shu. After the Five Titans carried the five bulls back to Shu, they found the five bulls were not gold but stone. But the road to Old Shu had been opened up by the Five Titans! The King of Qin feared the Five Titan's power but could not attack Old Shu, so he made the honey trap, sending 5 beautiful girls to the King of Old Shu. When on the way back to Old Shu, the Five Titans found a huge snake going into a hole. They wanted to capture the snake but the snake was too huge; finally the entire mountain crumbled in a great landslide and the Five Titans and the 5 girls all died. Then Qin attacked Old Shu without any worries. Old Shu was over.

Six times a day: Buddhism divides a day into 6 parts: Dawn, Noon, Dusk, Early Evening, Mid-night, The Wee Hours. This statement is from India.

Shang and Zhou: they are the ancient ages before Xia.

Shang: (1600-1046 BC) is the first Dynasty that had literary records. Before Shang, the history of Hua Xia amounts to only tales or archaeology. During the history of Shang, its capital had to be moved 14 times, finally settling down in Yin (Yang City in Henan Province). At the great battle of Mu-Ye, Shang was defeated by Zhou.

Zhou: (1046-256BC) is the longest Dynasty in Hua Xia history. Its history is divided into two periods, the West Zhou Dynasty and the East Zhou Dynasty. It's the first Dynasty which promoted the system of hereditary nobility, which caused the revolutionary war in the Spring and Autumn and the Warring States period. When West Zhou destroyed the King of You in 771 BC, King Ping moved the capital to East Zhou, to Luo Yi (in Henan Province). In 770-476 BC, some big vassal states started swallowing up some small vassal states, and the Spring and Autumn period opens its curtains. It is ruled by a succession of powerful chief princes of this period. Five famous chiefs appeared in sequence: Duke Huan of Qi, Duke Xiang of Song, Duke Wen of Jin, Duke Mu of Qin and King of Zhuang In Chu. The Spring and Autumn period (475-221 BC) gave way gradually and the Warring States period began. Seven vassal states start to eliminate each other around 256 BC. The last Emperor of Nan in Zhou appealed to six vassal states (Yan, Zhao, Chu, Qi, Han, Wei) to send armed forces to resist the attacks of Qin, but no States answered. The capital was occupied by Qin and the Emperor was killed by the soldiers of Qin. The Zhou Dynasty was over.

Yan Zi Kan: a temple located on the path from Shaanxi to Sichuan Province.

43. Spontaneously Writing: Six Poems

(1)
There's an extremely conceited fellow in Chu country –
He is absolutely absent from any thinking or worry,
In his unfastened tunic, with long, disheveled hair,
Walking and singing at Nan Mo…people stare…
Confucius speaks to him, but can't encourage
Him by virtue and justice, the wisdom of the sage.
It's unnecessary to ask Heaven why he needs
To play Rang and then laugh at the noble deeds
Of the ancient persons Bo Yi and Shu Qi –
Dead? How can he say that? How can they be?

(2)
There is an elder with long grey hair, living
At times in a poor village house. Of course,
Through the off season, he would be preparing
His fine wine and inviting his neighbours.
They chat, sitting or standing under the eaves
Of his thatched cottage. Everything there relieves.
Don't think dressing in coarse cloth is a problem for him –
Even using garden palms to bind his feet is fine with him.
He's living easy, bringing up descendants… has never seen
The streets of the renowned big city…He says: There've been
Five ancient emperors and three kings – very great, even
These have all been called, since antiquity, Sons of Heaven:
Bury the hatchet into yielding space: quite…
After all is said and done, which way is right?

He says: When you are pleased with yourself, even though
You're in a temporary place, you are very happy. And so,
Staying in your one field for life you do consider vulgar –
We should spend our lives without any restraints, and go
Sturdily spend out the rest of our lives, be they near or far.

(3)
Sincerely, I would wish to join you there,
In the Mount Tai Hang monastery environs,

Keeping the hours allotted to monks, where…
But I couldn't, yet, with all my…hesitations.

You ask me why I still have to stick handle
My worldly affairs – my little family bundle –
My younger sister growing up day by day,
My brother yet unmarried (around home to stay?)

Traditionally, my family has been poor,
My official's income inadequate, unsure.
Though I usually don't have any savings,
I truly want to fly, to spread my wings.
Yet I hesitate to become a monk – I might
Look back at the world in secret delight.
Where I'm at now, there's a tower nearby
Where whistles old Sun Deng, who is wise.
There's a place another sage left in a muddle,
Only a few miles from here as the crow flies,
And there's an old friend there in the middle.

Greediness and desire are fading day by day
Zen and silence dwell in their fastness day by day…
I'll go off in a flash and I'll be swaggering –
There's no fearful need to wait for aging!

(4)
Tao Qian doesn't discipline his natural ignorance –
Indulging in his wine's the only thing for him that's sure.
His official position he resigns and gives offence.
Then somehow his family seems to be getting poor,
And even drink money seems to have run out the door.

On September ninth (it's Elders Day, the Double Nine),
He only carries chrysanthemums (no chrysanthemum wine).

"If someone gives me wine…" gyrates – his only plan.
And as hoped for, here comes someone: an old man
To see him, wearing white and bearing a wine can.
His drunken happiness never knew

If wine had arrived by litre or by dou
Later in the field, he shakes his clothes free of grime.
He sighs! Today, he has come up with one good time.

He's uncompromisingly unruled and consistently lost anew,
His coir rain cape and bamboo rain hat always go askew.
He almost passes out on the road home, braces himself
For a bad time, then sings a song to recover himself.
He doesn't really care about earning any kind of living,
Even though this fails to please the woman of his wedding.

(5)
Though only a girl from a Zhao country place,
Due to my fine harp-playing gifts, I controlled
A dancing position inside the Han Dan Palace.
My husband was the frivolous kind, but bold,
Learning to gamecock well, then entertain
The King's brother, the Duke of Qi. Using gold
For prostitutes, his expenses went insane.

When powerful families and honourable nobility
One after another came for my husband's frivolity,
And carriages with four stallions, not mares, were arriving
To fill our courtyard, it seemed our status was really thriving.

I notice actually refined people at hostels near to us,
The ones with the most impressive appearance taught
In the ways deriving from Confucius and Mencius.
I met someone so detached from ambition he's not
Bothered to be an official, though he's habitually studious.
From the Sage himself he received his education,
And mildly lives a poor life in study and meditation.

(6)
Now I am getting older, I tire of writing poetry,
Only heavy, stiff old age is accompanying me.
I was a poet in a previous life, writing absurd verse.
My predecessors were painters, for better or worse.
I couldn't give up my original game,

And was known by all the world in my day.
Basically, a name is only a name
But over my heart it still holds sway.

(1) *play Rang:* An ancient game, using one soil block or wooden stake or tile to hit others standing away about 20-30 meters. Whoever makes a hit is the winner. This game has been played in China for 4000 years.

(1) *Bo Yi And Shu Qi:* They are brothers who lived in the Shang Dynasty. They went to ask the Wu to oppose King Zhou of the Shang Dynasty, but the King of Wu didn't accept their entreaty, and when finally Zhou swept into Shang, these two brothers hid away in Mt. Shouyang, gathered firewood to support themselves, refused to eat the meals sent from Zhou, and finally starved to death at Shouyang Mountain.

(2) *Five ancient Emperors and three Kings:* the legendary Emperors before the Xia Dynasty were Three Kings: Suiren, Fuxi, and Shennong. Suiren drilled wood and made fire; Fuxi created The Eight Diagrams of the I Ching; Shennong taught people to farm, test herbs and create herbal prescriptions.

(2) *Five Emperors:* The Yellow Emperor (Huang Di) was first, then Zhuanxiang, then Ku, then Yao, then Shun. The Yellow Emperor compiled "The Yellow Emperor's Classic of Internal Medicine." Zhuanxiang encouraged people to take up farming, and he prohibited sorcery. Ku emphasized kindheartedness and equality. He was the first leader in the Huaxia Nation. Yao is Ku's son; he divided the year into four seasons and legalized voluntary abdication of the King for the good of the country. Shun is one of the founders of Chinese morality, and a founder of Huaxia civilization; he is an example of a great dutiful son. These Emperors were legendary Emperors; they were all tribal leaders and belonged to the Mongolian region (called the Huaxia Nation).

(3) *Sun Deng:* A famous hermit who was born in the Wei-Jin period; it is said he had great whistling skill. He understood classical music rhythms, and his whistle was like a phoenix song (they would come when he whistled). He went into seclusion at Mt. Xuanyang, and people called the place he used to whistle, "Whistle Hill." In China, Whistle Hill is located on Mt. Sumen near Baiquan, a town in Hui County in Henan Province.

(4) *1 dou:* ancient Chinese measurement equal to 10 litres.

(4) *Tao Qian (Tao Yuanming):* his nickname was Wu Liu. After resigning his official position, he spent a hermit life at Mount Zhongnan and he planted five

willow trees by his house. People called him Mr. Wu Liu (Mr. 5 Willow Trees). It became an idiom for a hermit.

(5) *Xu Bo:* a powerful, rich man who lived in the time of Emperor Xuan of the Han Dynasty. He was the stepfather of Emperor Xuan.

(5) *Shi Gao:* He was a powerful, rich man and a senior officer. Emperor Xuan's uncle was Shi Gao's father. These two were relatives of the Emperor or relatives of the Emperor's mother, grandmother or mother-in-law or grand mother-in-law (it is Wai Qi, which means Matrilineal). Later, the name Xu Shi became synonymous with elite.

(5) *Confucius (Kongzi):* (551-479 BC) he was born in the late Spring and Autumn period, in Lu State. He was an ancient philosopher and educator and created Confucianism. He developed the tutor atmosphere in China. He edited six sutras (poetry, books, rites, music, the I Ching, and Spring and Autumn). He emphasized benevolence, righteousness, rites (ceremonies), knowledge (wisdom), and faith. He wanted to recover the world principle of the early Zhou. He had 72 disciples. After he died, his disciples collected the teachings of Confucianism, creating the book, *The Analects of Confucius.*

(5) *Mencius (Mengzi):* He is an ancient ideologist, philosopher, politician, educator, and successor of Confucius. At the age of 100 years, Confucius died. Mencius was born in Zou State. He is the earliest person to emphasize that people are much more important than the King. He emphasized Benevolent Government Rule. Many of his teachings or speeches were collected in his book *Mencium* (Mengzi). The same as Confucius, he also emphasized the Six Behaviours but more emphasized Benevolence and Righteousness, and even said that filial duty is the first foundation of morality. He was very much influenced by his mother. In China, it's a very famous story how his mother educated him, moving three times to create a good environment for him. Much of his teaching is mentioned in elementary or junior high school.

44. Elegy for the Late Mrs. Fan of Nanyang

You got a fiefdom, Shi Mao, and rather something
More than kindnesses and favours from the King.
You'd go out in your state carriage, so spectacular,
With a guard of honour and the cavalry with sabres.
When the King used to go to the palace in full dress,
You always used to give him some words to express
How unwilling you were to part. The joy of you two together,
When he returned, you always paying respects to each other!
Now you have passed away, and the funeral drums cry –
Across the autumn city they reach, though sounding shaky.
We don't say you ever will come back, yet are impressed
As we still hear jade on the pendant from your old dress,
Dinging, dinging.

Shi Mao: a place located in Shenmu County in Shannxi Province.

45. About Yi Men

Still keeping China stuck in the era of the Warring States, they stir,
The Qin army, attacking castles, killing Generals one after another.
When they besiege the Citadel of Zhao, it creates an emergency
For the King of Wei, the King of Zhao's brother in law: you see,
He fears the power of Qin. No help comes for Zhao. No, sir.

But Lord Xin Ling of Wei wants to save Ping Yuan of Zhao.
He thinks of recruiting the hermit Hou Ying, who by now
Has for over 50 years guarded the castle gate with true know-how.

Xin Ling stops his horse cart, invites Hou Ying to get on
And respectfully holds the bridle for him. Prince Xin is one
Who actually respects the wise if they occupy a lower position –
His retainer Zhu Hai is a butcher at a humble butcher's shop,
Hou Ying has been a gate keeper at Yi Men, for the King a prop.

So when the Prince meets with the difficult circumstance
Not only do they generously offer good advice in advance
But even sacrifice their lives for him. For instance,
Hou Ying gives a secret message to Lord Xin Ling,
And to keep this secret, kills himself when sent homewards.
He wants to let the Lord know for sure one thing:
He now is over seventy, and needs, really, no rewards.

Lord Xin Ling: a prince of Wei State, he is the consanguineous younger brother of the King of Wei. His very famous story is about stealing the commander's seal to save Zhao State. He had two expeditions to try to combine with other countries to fight Qin and save his country, Wei. He is one of 4 famous lords in the Warring States period (Lord Xin Ling in Wei, Lord Ping Yuan in Zhao, Lord Meng Chang in Qi, Lord Chun Shen in Chu). He fostered many retainers, hangers on, but these retainers always gave him some good ideas or suggestions to help him. He was courteous but gathered suspicion from the King…finally he indulged too much in wine and beautiful girls and died of this behaviour. Eighteen years after he died, the Wei State was swept away by Qin. The Lord of Ping Yuan was his brother-in-law.

Lord Ping Yuan: A Prince of Zhao State, the King of Hui Wen's younger brother. He was a prime minister from the time of the King of Hui Wen to that of Hui Wen's Son – The King of Xiao Cheng. As same as Xin Ling, he also fostered over 1000 retainers. His very famous story is "Mao Sui Self-Recommended." Mao Sui was his follower for over 3 years. Compared with Xin Ling, the Prince of Ping Yuan ignored the common people and didn't find wisdom from Mao Sui. But he was brave to reform his mistakes. After he died, Zhao perished at the hands of Qin.

Hou Ying: a doorkeeper in the capital of Wei State. As a hermit, he gives Xin Ling an idea to help him save the Zhao State. The great hermit always hid himself in the city.

Zhu Hai: Hou Ying's friend – a butcher, he helped Xin Ling kill the commander Bi Fu and led Xin Ling, guiding the army to rescue the State of Zhao.

46. At Longtou

At the frontier, a young swordsman from Chang An
Climbs the garrison tower to watch the rise of War Venus.
The bright moon of Longtou differs from Lin Guan's.
The guard on duty this evening plays the flute just
As the old General who served in Guan Xi halts
His cart to listen, with tears, to the melancholy notes.
He has experienced hundreds of deadly battles
But still he lingers in this outpost so remote,
Though even his deputies have retired with medals
And have been rewarded with titles, like *Marquis*.
Of course, even though the famous warrior Su Wu
Returned after the campaigns of the great Han Dynasty
To become a minor officer like Dian Shu Guo from Xiong-Nu.
Although he held the envoy's flag to shepherd at Haixi,
The flag's braid has dropped, and its honour, too.

War Venus: also called the Tai Bai Star. In Taoism, it is a he, an immortal controlling Venus. It's also called Mars, administrator of war. This star is in one of the 28 constellations, and is the brightest star in the celestial body. Ancient people watched it to predict the outcome of wars.

Longtou: Mt. Long, located in Gansu Province.

Linguan: a place located in Sichuan province.

Guanxi: the region of west Tong and Hangu pass was called Guanxi in the Han and Tang Dynasties. It's in Shaanxi Province around the Wei River.

Su Wu: an officer in the Han Dynasty. His very famous story is called "Su Wu Shepherd." As an emissary, he went to Xiyu, a place Sino-barbarians occupied. But he was detained by Chan Yu, a King of the barbarians. They wanted to convince him to capitulate, but he refused. Finally, they sent him to Haixi, a remote place, to shepherd. After 19 years, he returned to Han and got a great welcome (but they only gave him a minor position: Dian Shu Guo).

Dian Shu Guo: an officer administering the business of foreign affairs in the Qin and Han Dynasties.

Xiong-Nu: Sino-barbarians, a horde nation. It is said they were descendants of the Hua Xia Nation. After the Xia era was over, part of the people moved to the north – Mt. A Er Tai and the highland, E Er Duo Si, presently in Xinjiang territory. They settled down there. It was a period of great prosperity (209-128 BC). Later, it was divided into Northern Barbarian and Southern Barbarian areas. The Southern Barbarians blended into the Han Nation, but the Northern Barbarians moved to West Asia (Turkey, and some eastern European countries). Accordingly, the Xia-Bei Nation rose abruptly, as the barbarians withdrew from their historical arena.

Haixi: A place located to the west of Qinghai Lake in Qinghai Province.

47. Yan Zhi

The great General star drops from Han Jia, forges his heroic fate.
He's off to the frontier, leaving from the Mingguang estate,
And the Emperor pushes his cart by Shuang Que at the palace gate.
At a banquet at Wu Ling many officers wish to bid him farewell.
He says good bye to the Gold Gate Palace and his family,
Puts himself into the frontier at Yumen Guan, by the Great Wall.
Comparing Wei Qing's or Huo Qubing's to his ability,
Might be to liken them to mere Generals of the Cavalry.
If one compares the contribution of even Er Shi, he would be
Only one among the number of the high Imperial Courts.
Among the Warring States, the country of Zhao Wei was rich
In brave soldiers, even lionhearted soldiers, Yan Zhi's resource,
The best one for a young heroic general, and he also had that which
Made getting vengeance on him only like Yue's old King tasting gall.
Drinking wine – like Guang Yu scraping his bones –
Won't hurt him. It only helps to treat his wounds.
When he goes out to battle, the weapons like Ji and Ge flashing all
Across the sky, the battle flags covered in desert dust, the sounds
Of battle drums pounding louder than even the turning sea waves,
The mighty noise of Jia shakes the moon above Tian Shan.
He wears the dress belt with the Kaylin pattern and saves
The Wu Gou swords he captured, rides to implement his plan
To attack the enemy cavalry on his precious Zi Liu horse, his sabre
Cutting an enemy officer's arm, chopping an enemy general's head,
When he comes back to his campus. His very brave soldiers, under
The noise of sky-raising battle can each produce a hundred dead.
The enemy's cavalry, seeing this, were some crying, all, distressed.
Asking soldiers to step into the fire is as hard as can be guessed,
Yet we know the greatest general makes all strategies unstressed.

Yan Zhi: A mountain located in Gansu Province in the Tang Dynasty, in the Sino-barbarian region.

Han Jia: The Milky Way.

Mingguang Palace: a palace where the Emperor treated the Generals who are to go to the frontier (Tang Dynasty).

Shuang Que: the two stone poles which stand in front of the Palace. The east one is called Dragon Que; the western one is Xuan Wu Que. (A Que is a stone pole.)

Wu Ling: five tombs of five Emperors and Queens of the Han Dynasty; it's far from Chang An, about 40 miles. In the Tang Dynasty it was also a place to send senior officers to the frontier.

Gold Gate Palace: the imperial court.

Er Shi (Li Guangli): his older sister married the Emperor of Wu in the Han Dynasty. As a relative of the Emperor, he became a General and led troops to fight the Sino-barbarians in Da-Wan Country (in the Xinjiang Region). He rode a thoroughbred horse, contributed to the Emperor's cause, and became a Marquis. He defended against the Sino-barbarians and won a great victory. Three times he fought the enemies: the first and second battles were great successes, but at the third battle he was overwhelmed and taken into barbarian territory as a captive. One year later he was killed, as an oblation.

Yumen Guan (Yumen Pass): located in Dunhuang City in Gansu Province. A pass connects the silk road, established in the Hanwu Age (the time of Emperor Wu in the Han Dynasty). The name Yumen Guan comes from a route that carried boulder sized jades.

Yue's old King tasting gall: an idiom about the King of Yue, Gou Jian. When his nation was destroyed by the King of Wu, he lay every day on firewood as his bed and tasted gall before his meals. He was always aware of the national humiliation, and ended by wiping out the state of Wu, and took revenge on its King. Then Wu State disappeared.

Guan Yu scraping his bones: Guan Yu was a great General in Shu Country in the Three Kingdoms period. He was injured by arrows once, and although his wounds healed, on rainy or cloudy days, the wounds often produced sores. He met a doctor who said the arrowheads had poison which had entered his bones, and he had to accept the treatment of scraping the bone to remove the poison. Guan Yu accepted this special treatment and drank wine at a meal with his friends as a painkiller. Even though he bled greatly, he remained unconcerned. Later, people made this story into a metaphor meaning a man who is very brave. In the present time, Guan Yu (Guan Gong) has become a god of wealth and The Patron Saint of War.

Ji and Ge: two kinds of ancient Chinese weapons, like axes or daggers on poles.

Jia: A musical instrument, a whistle made of reed, very similar to a bamboo flute. It is a northern musical instrument.

Tian Shan: one of 7 mountain chains in the world, crossing the Asian and European continents. It is located in the Xinjiang region and connects three other countries: Kazakhstan, Kyrgyzstan, and Uzbekistan. It's the furthest inland mountain chain in the world.

Wu Gou Sword: actually not a sword or a knife. It has a hook-like shape and is a deadly weapon, usually having one side or both sides as blades. As it was used in Wu and Yue States, it was called the Wu Gou Sword. It is now an idiom meaning Go to Battle.

Kaylin: fabled luck-bringing animal in ancient China, with the head of a dragon, body of an elk, tail of a bull, and hooves of a horse. The Kaylin pattern indicates a senior military officer.

Zi Liu: An esteemed Mongolian horse in ancient China with a white body and face alternating with purplish hair.

Step into the fire: an idiom meaning to pluck up your courage to do something.

the greatest general makes all strategies: this is an idiom from the book *Sun Zi War Craft,* referring to a man who knows that the best way to defend others is by using strategy (not war).

48. A Poem for Mr. Li Suiyang

I'm drinking to you, thinking of you, very sad –
You'll depart today from here, east of the castle.
The wheat gradually grows up, as it always has;
Pheasants fly up, pagoda trees shade your vessel –
From here to your far destination, Tong Guan,
You'll need to ride in this wagon continuously.
I am heartbreak…the state of Song is farther on,
Zhou is at the centre, in the south is Nan Huaiyi,
In the east is Qi Er. All the places make textile ribbon
And white silk, but the credit is very hard, siphoning
Between the wealthy traveler and local businessman.
When you see the famous five cereals slowly ripening
You'll get credit; go there to become an officer.
You should think about it, make many a consideration.
When the Emperor is sitting in the palace court, be sure,
He will put on the King's dress, the official high position,
And drink from the "yu shang," that special beaker . . .
The court meeting's over sounds the charming ding-ling for:
A new Imperial Yellow Paper, from the Eastern Chamber.
Gorgeous foppery is profligate in the palace's shining corridors,
But you are the best in the royal household, the most virtuous of all.
Of course, the first duty for you is sharing the worries of the Emperor –
Even common people would sacrifice to answer the Emperor's call,
And if the Emperor showed them kindness to the height of heaven?
Now it's leaving time: an imperial carriage with its bells encircling
Its girth arrives; an imperial flag (like the diligent King of Lu's) flying.
Next year it will be, when you come back to the capital, Chang An,
To report your work to the Emperor, but please don't forget our drinking,
And our parting, today, and please do not do anything imprudent –
Too many act recklessly when riches and honour are heaven sent.

Tongguan: a place located in Tongguan County in Weinan City in Shaanxi Province. The road can only be travelled with a horse cart as it's very difficult terrain. It has been the battlefield for troops since the time of Ancient China.

the state of Song: a state in the Spring and Autumn period. Its famous King was Xiang, King of Song.

Zhou: a pre-Qin Dynasty. (See footnote for poem 42.)

Nan Huaiyi: an ancient small region in Anhui in the Spring and Autumn period.

Qi Er: an ancient small region in Shandong in the Spring and Autumn period.

famous five cereals: hemp, wheat, millet, rye and rice. The specific five varied over time. When these crops start ripening, it is time to collect silk.

"yu shang": an ancient wine vessel with two handles like a bird's wings and sometimes three legs. Yu Shang means Bird Feather.

imperial carriage with its bells encircling its girth: the idiom is from the Book of Song, which tells of the King of Xuan in the Zhou Dynasty, who was very attentive to his imperial business. Even in the early morning he would wake up and go to court to await the official meetings. Wang Wei implies that the Emperor will concern himself about Li Suiyang anytime now.

(like the diligent King of Lu's): in the Spring and Autumn period, a new King was crowned in State of Lu. The situation was critical, as this small state constantly faced being swallowed up by larger nearby states. He used his diligence and intelligence to handle this very difficult situation and made a great success.

49. Climbing to The Pavilion at He Bei

Some households are down by Fu Yan;
The high pavilion, standing for the rest,
Hides from the clouds and fogs upon
This high level, facing directly west.
Contemplating the splendid setting sun,
I observe the distant river long reflect
The shadow of the great and dusky mountain.
By the shoreside, a few fires shine. I detect
That one lonely boat waits out there, moored.
Fishermen may return with the evening birds
As night blooms and falls open silently.
My heart moves like that river – wide, assured,
Comfortably full, large and leisurely.

Fu Yan: the name of a big rock in Hebei (presently Pinglu County in Shanxi Province). It is said that exemplary officer Fu Shui had stayed there before he became an officer.

50. Another Elegy for Mrs. Fan of Nanyang

You wore most gorgeous dresses and your cart
Would hide inside its pheasant feathers.
A fish skin body set your cart apart,
Your poems like maidens fair gave lively pleasures.
Mrs. Fan, your memory won't be overcome –
Now the Jia make low sobs with mourning flags –
They are crying to the placid prairie autumn.
You passed away, and the heart just sags:
When we return to Court, who will we see?
At the Imperial Gate, who will we be?

Jia: A musical instrument whistle made of reed. It's very similar to the bamboo flute. It belongs to a northern nation's music instruments.

51. For Chao Heng, as Mi Shu Jian, Ambassador to Japan

A vast sea, its boundary so far beyond
It hardly can be reached, they say –
Among its myriad creatures, a riddle it has spawned:
What is next to Jiuzhou, from Jiuzhou far away?
Of course, it's your own homeland, the country of Japan –
You'll cross those thousand miles, if I understand your plan.
During your trip, you'll guide your ship
Forward to The Sunrise State.
Filled with the wind, your sails equip
You to go forward to your fate,
To meet the turtle of legendary size,
Its huge body darkening the skies,
Red light bursting from its fishy eyes…
You brought here and planted your Japanese tree
But you're still lonely and miss Japan so much.
Between us now, two countries and a sea –
My friend, how can we keep in touch?

Chao Heng: a Japanese citizen who came to China in the Tong Dynasty era. His Japanese name was Abe no Nakamaro. As a diplomat to the Tang Dynasty, he passed the national exam there. Then he became an officer in the Tang Dynasty, staying on and eventually dying in China, although he tried to return to Japan. But a tremendous typhoon drove him back, and he was lucky to be alive.

Mi Shu Jian: an officer in charge of the imperial library.

Jiuzhou: another name, meaning Nine Regions, representing China. Since the Warring States period, this term was popular in China. This is an ancient Chinese geographic concept. It contained the regions of Ji, Yan, Qing, Xu, Yang, Jing, Yu, Liang, and Yong.

52. Pei Di and I Try to Visit Hermit Lv Whose House Is in Xinchang Li *(But We Don't See Him)*

It always isolates one from the world, peaches blooming…
We visited you, a hermit who lived in Liushi's south end.
We cautiously approached your gate, very unassuming,
Afraid to knock at your door, more respectful than a friend.
We really couldn't think of you, treat you, as a common bird,
But we can enjoy your garden bamboo without asking for you.
Your house and the mountain faced each other, we observed,
As if the mountain sat inside your house, one thing, not two.
The stream therefore seemed to run through the eastern wing
Of your house, and roundabout, far to the distant western pales.
Your blinds closed for many years, many books you're writing;
Your pine's bark, its rind, has grown hard like dragon scales.

Liushi: a suburb of Chang An.

treat you as a common bird: as a mediocre person. The idiom is from the Book, *A New Account of the Tales of the World.* From the Three Kingdoms period in Wei country, Ji Kang and Lv An were very good friends. One day Lv An visited Ji Kang but Ji Kang had gone out. Ji Kang's brother Ji Xi was at home and came to meet Lv An, but Lv An didn't enter the home, only inscribed the word "Feng" (Phoenix) on the gate. Ji Xi thought it was praise of he himself and was very happy. In fact, the ancient Chinese word combined two characters Fan (common) and Niao (bird), making a crack at Ji Xi.

enjoy your garden bamboo: this idiom comes from the book, *Jin Statement.* One day, the great calligrapher Wang Xizhi discovered an official's beautiful bamboo grove, entered, and stayed there with whistle and song. The owner appeared and invited him to stay and sit awhile, but Wang Xizhi didn't care to do so. Eventually, he did return and the owner closed the gate and served some drinks. They became good friends.

dragon scales: they symbolize aging but, at the same time, keeping fit into longevity.

53. About the Queen of Xi

Don't think you could have given me
The gift of your special love, ardently,
And I would have forgotten my old grace.
Look, with tears upon my sincere face,
I appreciated the flowers you sent through.
I even didn't talk down to you –
And I am a King of Chu.

Queen of Xi: A Queen of the Xi State, also known as Mrs. Peach Blossom, so beautiful that the King of Chu (Wen King) sent his troops to sweep away the State of Xi. To save the life of her husband, she had to become a Queen of Chu, but she still yearned for her former husband. She didn't speak to the King of Chu for three years.

King of Chu: he invaded and destroyed the Kingdom of Xi, and he wanted to kill the King of Xi and take the Queen to be his own wife as she was a great beauty. To save her husband's life, she accepted the forced marriage to the King of Chu. However, she genuinely missed her former husband.

Wang Wei wrote this poem for a Prince of Qi who bribed a chief of a nearby family and bought one of his wives (also very beautiful) to be his concubine. One year later, he asked the chief to come visit, and was so moved by seeing their love for each other, the chief and his former wife, he gave the concubine back.

54. Cousin Fan Journeys to Huainan

Reading books while shooting or on horse rides,
Touring down to Huaiyin with your shining sword…
Huaiyin sees a lot of young guys with thick hides;
You meet them from a thousand miles away or more,
If you have a loyal or noble friend. It's hard to be a hermit
Unless you're wise enough to live without a public face.
The strange island of Jiuzhou where recluses live out of it
Has a hostel away in the mountain, a deep hiding place.
You? Ordered to sail on a reed mat boat on a big crusade
Against those islanders – they'll all be arrested and quelled
And you'll come back to meet the Emperor, career made.
You'll be invested and granted your reward – a lot of gold.
Suddenly you'll think of your homeland and want to return…
Then you'll entertain the thought to live a hermit's life.
I imagine the scenario when being a hermit's your concern –
The weather is cold, an islet in the reeds is your cold wife,
The sun is bathing the forest like a dream in a cloud,
The maple leaves drop under the castle as you come
To the Huai River – you hear the anvil speak aloud,
The washer-maids beat the clothes to it in autumn.
I'll send you to the main gate to leave the city,
I'll hear your horse cart faintly creaking far into the plain…
I am disconsolate like the barren Xinfeng tree –
All the birds have disappeared; only emptiness remains.

55. To My Younger Brother Jin *(When I'm Saying Goodbye to Master Wen Gu at Mount Song)*

I will take off the robes of seclusion and I will return
To the official life (as an officer) in my next life-stage,
And leave you, Master Wen Gu; you are a modern sage–
Not only are you a person who's secluded in the mountain
But also, you had the idea to carry the moon that shone
Above the pine trees, in the old time when we were on
Mount Song, and appreciated the clouds at the dawn
And in the evening glow; and lived in the place where
Doors opened on nearby Ying Yang, sleeping, or watching
The birds flying up or down, or eating our meals there
By the rock, or by the spring waters, our thirst quenching.
If you want to trim yourself, to seclude in youth is fine.
The great way would be rather to give up external things.
My brother Jin, to become a high officer you incline…
Wen Gu became a Master, an older friend of mine:
No matter what may become of our refuge or of us, we
Merely sweep our poor courtyard out when we are free.

Jin (Wang Jin): Wang Wei's younger brother, whose official position was higher than Wang Wei's, that of a Prime Minister. He helped the Emperor calm the Rebellion of An and Shi (Wikipedia has details) and helped Wang Wei when he was in disgrace with the Emperor and was in danger of being executed. He was also a poet.

Master Wen Gu: refers to Tang Zhisheng, a very famous monk of the Vajrayana school in Tang Dynasty times. He lived on Mt. Song in Henan Province.

Yingyang: a town at Yingyang in Dengfeng County in Henan Province.

56. Mount Hua

Mount Hua, called Xi Yue where it ranges
To the west, its snow like pillows on the sky,
To dark black the blue sky it changes,
In a hundred-mile radius, cold and high –
Even the sun seems cold under its boundless shadow.
Hua Yin City sits by this mountain, a gloomy crow.

The sky and earth once were one, old texts let you see.
Then a huge spirit – the river god – was born, broke free,
Its right foot smashing out square rocks,
Its left hand chopping with all nature's power,
Earth and sky separated by its shocks.
Into the Eastern Sea ran the Yellow River;
Into the Western Mountain the spirit then faded, still strong.
This mountain manfully guards the Qin-Jing (Guanzhong).

You our Emperor, carry the grace that contains all things on Earth.
You, Emperor, have supreme virtue over all creatures that take
birth.
Now the God of Heaven stands for a declaration from your fame.
Mount Hua awaits a title – from you the gold standard is coming.
The Immortals expect you to give him a permanent lucky name.
It's not only you who's offering the new name to Mount Yun Ting.

Xi Yue: another name for Mt. Huashan, one of the 5 sacred mountains of China. It is located in the southwest of Hua Yin County, near Xi'an City in Shaanxi Province. It's a doorway from the northwest to central China (Zhong Yuan). This mountain reaches to heaven and falls to earth, steep on all sides. It's very precipitous and nearly impossible to climb to its summit. It's called *The Steepest Mountain in China.*

Qin- Jing: it indicates Guanzhong: a region between Hangu Pass and Dasan Pass. It is also called the Guanzhong Plains or the Wei River Region.

Mt. Yun Ting: another name for Mount Tai. The King of Yan visited and gave the mountain a lucky name: Yun (Cloud); then the Yellow Emperor visited there, and gave it the name of Ting (Upright). Since then, Dong Yue Mountain, Mount Tai (East Mount Tai) has been called Mt. Yun Ting.

57. A Poem for Ding Yu, Who Lives in a Farmhouse

You still live in seclusion and you still live a reclusive lifestyle.
I have a thought to follow you – to become a hermit, though
You know when you're an official, you do statements all the while.
If you resign from the official world, you become interesting, no?
In the morning when you hear the cock crow, you know everyone
Will prepare to do something that they know they should do:
Farmers take their meals to the fields where cultivation's done;
Farmers' women get up sewing, stitching…embroidering, too.
When you open the window, you know to get into dress,
When reading books, you know how to select certain paragraphs.
Sometimes you read your poems about seclusion, ah yes,
Or you write 'Fu' about your life of leisure, just for laughs.

When weather's fresh, you can watch sunshine from the city walls,
Soaking nearby suburbs. When cloudy, the elms and mulberries
Look old. When shadows cover Xiaoyuan City, when night falls,
At the Wei river, its owl light makes a subtle shining in the trees.
You only manage your house and the village well's shelter –
You appreciate it silently, though – is any trouble upon you?
We have the same way, that we never forget each other.
It's very hard to meet again if different corners turn into
Our paths of life. Right now, we say goodbye unwillingly,
But I hope we will meet again in some lucky hours,
And at that happiest time, we will again, and gratefully,
Appreciate the fragrance of all the little flowers.

*you become interesting, no?:*mentioned his friend interest in spending a hermit life.

Fu (vigorous prose poems): a style of writing in Ancient China that combines essays and poetry. It emphasizes writing that sparkles and rhymes and takes advantage of a scene to express a writer's emotion. This style begins in the Warring States period and the time of its greatest popularity was in the Han Dynasty, so it is also called "Han Fu." It had a variety of styles: short Fu, literary Fu, Fu in the style of Li Sao, prose poems and principle poems.

58. Offering a Meal to a Monk from Mount Fufu

I understand (the more old age and I get into it),
The truth of my commitment, to peace and quiet.
More and more I keep a distance from the human.
Now I meet a monk who comes from a far mountain.
I sweep my humble house well in advance.
The master comes from the clouds' very summit,
And visits my poor house as if by chance.
I will stuff straw cushions, make the meal, cook it.
In fragrant incense we will read our Buddhist tomes.
When the lights turn on we'll know the daytime ends,
We'll play the Qing and feel when night just comes;
We'll even enjoy loneliness, as enlightened friends.
Then after our day's full span, so leisurely and fun –
Why consider going home? (I do ask this one),
As all the world's bodies just make an old illusion!

Qing: a musical instrument used in Buddhist temples when they read sutras or practice Buddhist dharma.

59. Suffering from Hot Weather

The red sun colours half the sky and down on earth,
The fiery clouds have made volcanos of the mountains.
All the woods or grasses roll, as if a burning re-begins.
All the streams and rivers dry up from waters' dearth.
Even wearing light, thin robes I still feel gross and heavy.
Staying in the woods but still lacking the cool and shady,
I cannot bear to touch the mats of bamboo or of straw,
And several times a day the coarse cloth needs a wash.

My thought jumps from this universe, open-minded, vast –
Though the wind comes from ten thousand miles away,
Sweeping out all worries like a river washes dirt in play:
I'm still worried for my body, when I self-reflect at last –
I find I haven't grasped an enlightenment that will stay.
Then suddenly I feel I understand: I'm going to cast
The gates of sweet dew specifically for the way
I enjoy, embrace, the cool, refreshing wind today.

gates of sweet dew: Nirvana.

60. A Song to Li Ling

There's a famous General, General Li of the Han Dynasty,
Whose past three generations – from grandfather to grandson –
Were all genial to the military. Li Ling, when but a child, he
Wished to have not one good deed to his country left undone.
When he was a youth, he became most vigorous –
He rode his horse to the frontier, beyond the great wall
And charged though to the enemy Chan Yu's fortress.
Banners and flags lined up for the enemy's fall –
How much sorrow when the xiao and drum sound
With the dreaded setting sun sinking in the desert…
The battle's noise buried into the smoke all around.
He bravely leads his soldiers: they'd been ordered
By their General to destroy the overbearing enemy.
Since the King's order to destroy the enemy, in a sense.
How is it possible he is merely an attendant of Li Guangli?
However General Li Ling loses the King's reinforcements,
And is forced to surrender. Then he meets shame and care,
Is sent to live in a Mongolian yurt, though dedicated to the King
Since he was a child! How could he imagine he'd sit there!
In his heart, he wanted to attempt to surrender everything
And take the chance to serve the royal Han, face every dare.
Now the one person who could understand him, Zi Qing,
Has gone. He can only crane his neck to look for Zi Qing –
Who vindicate him? – only Zi Qing?!

*Merely attendant of Li Guangli:*this refers to Li Ling not only a vice General to assistant Li Guangli defend the Sino-barbarians but also he did their own achievement.

Chan Yu: the name of the King of the Sino-barbarians.

Zi Qing: the other name of Su Wu, who was exiled by the Sino-barbarians to be a shepherd in a remote territory. Li Ling, a fellow Han subject, but one who surrendered, helped Zi Qing through hard times, asking his wife to send Zi Qing a supply of food. This saved his life. When Zi Qing went back to Han and they said good bye, Li Ling watched him and sighed: nobody understood his feelings. He had to stay with the barbarians, but his heart was still actually with the Han Dynasty.

61. A Visit to Mr. Jia's house, Near Mount Taiyi

From in the old days when I lived a cloistral life,
In the mountain mist and clouds and soft twilight,
I remember a neighbour of ours, Mr. Zhi Zi…
We used to buy his wine made from the pine tree,
And the bamboo skins we used as clasps for hair.
We climbed the mountain jungle with all care
And crossed through all the rock caves far up there.
We collected herbs, winter or spring, no matter…
But the King misunderstood me to be a Taoist – then
He called me up to service under Mr. Can Yu Chen.
The King always worried, if an elixir'd been refined,
He'd become an immortal like the late Mr. Zi Yang,
Earlier than I. Dying before I did did haunt his mind.
Now, Zhi Zi, you have mortality – your ideologies stopped.
Now that I face your house, with newly sorrowful thought,
I see you had a sharp sense of integrity, tolerant and mature,
And a contrary intelligence that let you keep your nature.
Now I can only face the double springs in some despair –
When I revisit the mountain, there'll not be my host there.

Zhi Zi: ancient Chinese words for the person this poem mentions Jia Yi (200 - 168 BC), a famous litterateur and politician. His essays became an important influence for many other writers. His thinking was very complex: not only enriched by Confucianism but also Taoism and Legalism. However, his highest reputation was as a fortune-teller. He didn't get the Emperor's appreciation; the Emperor was only concerned about conferring with him about the soul, or ghosts. He got a position as the prince's tutor; unfortunately, the prince of Liang died by an accident, falling off his horse when with Jia Yi. Jia felt very sad and guilty, and finally wore himself away with grief and depression, dying at only 33 years of age.

Can Yu Chen: the name of an official, whose main duty was to be the assistant of the minister.

Mr. Zi Yang: it is said he lived in the Han Dynasty. He went to Mt. Meng and met an immortal–Xuan Men Zi, who taught him how to gain longevity. Later, Zi

Yang was reported to having been seen flying through the heavens in daytime. The inference is: immortality!

Mt. Taiyi: its other name is Mt. Zhongnan or Mt. Nan. This mountain is a cradle of multiculturalism in China. It contains the culture of longevity, Daoism, Buddhism, filial culture, the culture of Zhong Kui (a person who was famous for stopping ghosts), and the culture of the god of wealth. It belongs to the massif of Mt. Qinling. Wang Wei had stayed there and lived a hermit lifestyle.

The double Springs: one refers to the Taiyi spring or Taiyi pool that belongs to a mountain lake. It is said Ziyang Zhenren and Jia Yi had stayed by the lake to perform alchemy. The other spring refers to the netherworld dwelling place of the dead. Wang Wei expresses his feeling that on one hand the spring is still running, on the other hand, humans vanish. Wang Wei's two springs: one is reality and the other, illusion.

62. Offering Some Wine to Mr. Pei Di

I'm offering to you some wine, please relax and worry not,
As human relationships, like the winds, blow both cold and hot.
Even the best friend, who can maintain a friendship until aging
Still will take to hand the sword, for protection from the raging,
Or for a powerful and distinguished person, living at the Red Gate,
Laughing at you, dusting his cap off, awaiting a nod from the State.
The grass is always getting green, due to the arriving rain,
The spray wants to bloom but a cold Spring returns again.
The world affairs are not worth mentioning – no big deal;
I would rather lie on the mountain and add an extra meal.

Pei Di: a poet in the Tang Dynasty. He was Wang Wei's friend and lived with Wang Wei at the Wang River villa. He wrote much poetry with Wang Wei and was also known as a pastoral landscape poet.

take to hand the sword: refers to anyone angry and prepared to attack. This idiom comes from the book, *Shi Ji:* Mao Sui was a hanger-on following the prince of Ping Yuan on his visit to Chu, to ask Chu to save Zhao when the State of Qin attacked Zhao. The King of Chu did not want to help Zhao, but Mao Sui took to hand the sword against the King of Chu; and so it happened that the King of Chu came to accept that it was his duty to help Zhao. Later, people made this an idiom for a very angry person.

Red Gate: also called a Zhu Men, a symbol of wealth.

dusting his cap off: ready to take an official position.

63. A Poem for Prince's Qi's Contest: *When We Visit Yang's Villa*

Back in the Han Dynasty was the time when Yang Xiong
Was teaching knowledge, and the nobility of Huainan,
Used to have the responsibility to bring wine to drink.
Now we're stationed here, enjoying it, as one may think,
Then we find changed so quickly the songs of twittering birds…
We've sat too long, only aware of all the thickly fallen flowers.
And so we cross the winding path, the candle glimmering;
After the forest, the light, as if jade, disperses, shimmering.
In the early morning when we come back, the gate is still
Closed, but with song and Sheng, we march on with a will.

Yang Xiong: or Zi Yun, was a philosopher, writer, and linguist in the Han Dynasty. He wrote many essays (called Fu) emphasizing that humans are a combination of virtues and evils. He realized Xuan (the mysterious)–a Great Way (like the Tao) for humans to follow.

the nobility of Huainan: one name or title for the nobility in Ancient China. This poem nods towards one Liu An, a prince in the Han Dynasty who had written a very famous book, *Huainan Zi*. He often talked to Yang Xiong about Yin (negative) and Yang (positive) and the five elements (wood, fire, earth, gold, and water).

Sheng: a wind instrument with at least a dozen reeds rising from a bowl at the base, and a mouth pipe at an angle.

64. A Stay in Zhengzhou

In the morning, to the town of Zhou I say goodbye,
To later lodge at Zheng, under that very evening's sky.
Only a houseboy's with me, no partner is close –
It's strange – I couldn't see the homes of Wan Luo,
And in autumn's incessantly-falling rains, to me,
The plains look desolate and definitely gloomy.
Farmers come in from their fields out on the plains;
The village boys are still out herding in the rains.
In the east of the village, where the waters drain,
Sits the farmers' land, seasonal crops surrounding
Their dwellings, summer swarms of insects droning.
The corn millets' quietude is ripped – a bird's cry.
Tomorrow I'll pass across the Jing River. But for
My last night, I'll stay over at Jin valley garden, indoors.
This time when I go there – how can I say – I sigh:
To save a little salary in these times I have to go
To places very far and poor, if you must know.

Zhou: refers to the Zhou Dynasty. Please see the footnote of poem 42.

Zheng: a state in the Spring and Autumn period. Its territory was located in the middle of Zheng. In this state lived a very famous person – Lie Tse (Liezi), who wrote the well known eponymous book, *Lie Tse* (Liezi).

Wan Luo: an ancient town's name. Wan refers to Nanyang City. Luo refers to Luoyang City. Both are in Henan Province.

Jing River: its head is in Mt. Gao-Zhu in Yingyang County in Henan Province. Take Zhengzhou City as a boundary of the upper reaches of the Jing River – the tail water is called the Jia-Lu River.

Jin valley garden (Gold valley garden): an ancient place name. It's located near Luoyang City. It was said in the Jin Dynasty to be a garden of Shi Chong's, and is a symbol of wealth.

65. After Reading "Thinking of Home When Looking at far Xi Lou," by Shijun Wulang

When I climb the Xi Lou and gaze from its highest side,
I always think of my hometown – my sadness I can't hide –
Even by the edge of heaven, homesickness never ends.
How many times in dreams, I walk back the thousand miles,
Through to the window sill, as if I see the many thousands
Of the households in my own hometown all the while.
Now we become passers-by, brief, unknown strands.
We're spending our dim lives far from the city,
Disconsolate and well out of range of any ferry.
Like a single line of smoke rising far from you,
You are a great talent (you can make Han Fu),
But when you think of home, the feeling is the same
As mine – a minor official's, in the government game.
You climb the famous high pavilion of far Xi Lou,
But can only observe the sky as clouds pass through,
While the heaven of sky-emptiness is what is for you.

Shi Jun: an official name for a Governor of a Province in Ancient China. Wu Lang is a personal name.

66. Sending Off Zu San at Qizhou

We just have smiles when we meet,
And when we part, we start to tease.
When I made the dinner for your departure,
I was so much in sadness, feeling all unsure.
Then I returned to the desolate castle with a tear.
It’s so cold, the faraway mountain’s very clear.
In the dusk, the river's water is fast-moving.
I thought of just untying the boat's tow rope,
But you’ve gone far away, outside my scope.
I stand by the ferry, looking for you, looking…

67. A Poem for the Hanshi Festival at River Fan

I am on the board of Guangwu Castle in this late spring.
As a returnee, I stand by the north shore of River Wen with tears.
I see the flower falling silently, hear a hatchling twittering.
As well, I watch men cross the river under their green wickers.

When Wang Wei wrote this poem, he had just received a new order from the Emperor to leave his exiled place, Jizhou [close to the Wen River] and return to Chang An, and was to pass through Luoyang [close to the Fan River] on the way.

Hanshi festival: a festival deriving from a story of the Spring and Autumn period. Before Zhong Er (a King of Jin State) became a King, he was exiled to other countries. His secretary, Jie Zhitui, followed him devotedly, even, when they were starving, cutting some meat from his own leg to feed Zhong Er. After Zhong Er became King, Jie Zhitui didn't accept the King's grace, but went with his mother to a secluded mountain to live there humbly. The willful King had this mountain burnt to force him out, but tragically, Jie Zhitui was killed in the fire. In his memory, the King ordered this day to be a day when all fires, even cooking fires, were prohibited in the State of Jin.

River Fan: ran through to Old Guangwu Castle (presently to the northeast of Mt. Guangwu, Yingyang County in Henan Province). This castle is divided into two parts, east and west.

River Wen: the head is in Yiyuan County in Shandong Province. It belongs to a tributary of a tail of the Yellow River.

68. Watching Someone Who's Leaving Home

There's a lane filled in with carts' green wickers –
There, the relatives say goodbye to each other.
The son likes to wander; he'll go on his way
(He likes the old countries of Yan and Zhao)
But his elderly parents, at home they will stay.
If he didn't travel so long he wouldn't now
Be escaping supporting his whole family's life.
But when he pushes off, he'll bring in full worry.
Merely, he whispers to a brother, or a wife,
"Let them look after their parents." And he'll curry
Favour with his neighbour most affectionately.
They'll drink a toast by the castle gate, and hence
He will separate from his relatives and friends.
He catches up to his partners with tears – he feels! –
As sorrowfully forward roll the heavy wheels.
The cart has gone but his parents still stand there,
Looking at wheel tracks in the dirt, dust in the air…
Actually, I too have to leave home for a long time.
Tears come down, rob me, though they're mine.

69. A Joyful Poem for a Rock

A lovely rock's close to the spring,
The weeping willow is kissing
My now-full wineglass, furthermore.
If you say the spring wind is not for
Anything making any sense at all,
Why by its blowing do flowers fall?

70. For My Siblings, a Poem from the Mountain

Here in the mountain retreat I am, yes,
With my fellow Buddhist disciples,
In groups to do Zen or read the sutras…
I think of you, and where you live, too–
How from the castle or city around you,
All you can see of our mountain retreat
Are the clouds drifting, distant and neat.

71. Pre-minister Zhang Now Lives in Jingzhou

Where can I find the one for whom I'm yearning?
Toward faraway Jingmen my melancholy's staring.
Although I had talent, nobody recognized it,
So when you gave me favour, I never forgot it,
But now, I hear you are demoted to Jing Zhou –
Back to the farmers' humble fields I traced you.
In the old village, plant and cultivate something.
Oh, I watch the geese v-forward to the faraway,
But it's impossible that they convey my missing
One who now in old Jingzhou town must stay.

Pre-minister Zhang: Refers to Zhang Jiuling,who promoted Wang Wei to an official position; after which, Wang Wei's official life was tightly connected to Zhang. After Zhang was demoted to Jingzhou, Wang Wei wrote this poem in sympathy.

Jingmen: also called Jingzhou. Its present place is Jiangling County in Hubei Province.

72. A Cry to Meng Haoran

Oh my friend, you just have gone–
It's as if the Han River ran away.
I will be arriving in Xiang Yang,
And I would ask the very city today:
Where I can find you? Called yourself old Xiang Yang, yes?
You passed away; your hometown Cai Zhou is emptiness.

Meng Haoran: a famous poet of the Tang Dynasty, Wang Wei's close friend. The same as Wang Wei, he is also a representative of pastoral landscape poetry. This style was called "Wang-Meng."

73. Sending Off Municipal Officer Yuwen to Xuancheng

The mountain-drifting of the clouds is desolate –
I sit inside the boat awhile and come to appreciate.
As if I hear the Xijiang brass band playing for me,
The water's sound surrounds the autumn sky so clearly.
You're posted to the place that's called the land's end,
And so bleakly its moon shines; cold waves spread…
However, I believe in your ability, tread there well,
And pray for luck – go inside the Jingting Temple.
Then you'll settle down the many problems, I bet,
Like a crafty fisherman untangles and unties his net.
Where can I send to you, my acute missing of you?
The south wind blows the Wu Liang, yet connects us, too.

Xijiang: the upper stream of the Yangtze River.

Jingting temple: located at Mt. Jing Ting (near Xuan City in Anhui Province). The god of this Taoist temple was called Mr. Zi Hua Fu.

Wu Liang: an object made of chicken feathers, as an anemoscope (instrument for wind direction) usually tied on the poop.

74. Qiu Wei Is Sent to Jiangdong After He Fails His State Examination

You are unhappy about failing state examinations. I empathize.
Again, it's time for wicker cart tops turning green, you realize.
Your hard experience causes me to think of Su Qin's mess,
Who went to Qin as a persuader, and used up his allotment.
Like him you went to Chang An, exhausting all expenses.
But I believe when you come back to your hometown, then
You will succeed in the future, and like Su Qin, turn again
Your grey hair back to black. I know you will come back to
Your hometown, walk along your home grounds at Tai Hu,
And to support your life, you have (though it's challenging)
A little property, about 3 Mu…probably I'll be apologizing;
I know your ability's like Mi Heng's, but it's impossible that
I imitate the career of Kong Rong, too irritating to the King:
I can't recommend you. As imperial censor, I'm ashamed about
that.

Qiu Wei: a friend of Wang Wei's, born in Jiaxing County, Zhejiang Province. He tried but failed several times to pass the state examination. He succeeded at last and became a senior officer.

Jiangdong: refers to the eastern section of the Yangtze River. It belonged to the Old Yue and the Wu States in the Spring and Autumn period, presently Zhejiang, Jiangsu, and Anhui Provinces.

Su Qin: born in East Zhou, his great achievement was combining 6 states into one anti-Qin state. At the beginning, no state would accept his unity proposals, and when his expenses were almost exhausted he had to return to his hometown, where his family and relatives all laughed at him. Then through reading, he found out about vertical integration. One year later, he made a tour to the State of Yan and finally persuaded its King to accept his proposal. Subsequently he persuaded the five other states, and the 6 states made an organization to resist Qin. He became a Minister of the 6 States. He became a great success.

Tai Hu: Tai Lake, one of the five largest freshwater lakes in China, located in Jiangsu Province crossing over Zhejiang and Jiangsu provinces. The area is beautiful scenery surrounded by mountains and water.

Mu: a unit of area measurement in China, one Mu being equal to 666.6667 square metres.

Mi Heng: a writer who was born in the Three States Period. He was rich in literary talent, but his narrow-minded tendencies led him to be killed by the Emperor's family. He died at only 26 years of age.

Kong Rong: a very famous writer in later East Han, very intelligent. His descendent was Confucius. When he was 4 years old, he and his older brother were given a pear to eat, divided in two, and he already understood to yield the larger section of the pear to his older brother. But in government, his outspoken personality brought Prime Minister Cao Cao's dislike and even hatred. Finally he was killed by Cao Cao, at the age of only 56 years. There is an interesting article about Cao Cao in Wikipedia.

75. Sending Off Xing Ji, Posted to Guizhou

The brass-bound band, now so noisy at Jingkou,
The boats sailing forward to Dongting Lake,
Floating, rowing, sailing, onward then to take
Folk – and you – passing by Zhejin and Chi'an, too:
Your destination at the setting sun you can appreciate,
The shine on the lake will glow, become a whiter colour;
During the rising tide the whole sky and earth…a fate
As if dying…dark blue…but still there's something more.
I hope you post there, recover the clear political state,
Like Meng Chang got the pearls developing at Hepu.
And the good royal court emissary star will be you.

Guizhou: Guilin City in Guangxi Territory

Jingkou: Zhenjiang City in Jiangsu Province

Dongting Lake: it is located in Hunan Province, one of the Five Freshwater Lakes of China.

Zhejin: a mountain hill in the northwest of Fanchang County in Anhui Province.

Chi'an: a mountain in Liuhe County in Jiangsu Province.

Meng Chang: an officer in the Han Dynasty. Before he moved to Hepu, many pearl-fishermen feared that the greedy officials would rob them, and they all moved to other regions and Hepu became a very depressed place. Meng Chang came to Hepu and reformed the policies and arrested the greedy officers. Then the pearl-fishers returned to Hepu and the pearl business recovered very well.

Hepu: a famous pearl-producing location in Guangdong Province.

emissary star: it is said if the King sends someone somewhere, it's like a star moving.

76. Joyful Poems for My Brother, Zhang Wu

(1)
When you, my brother, were a hermit at Dong Shan
You always kept a pure heart, away from the ambition.
Even late in the morning, you still lay in your bed
Until at noon you heard the clock ring by your head.
Then the scene – eating lunch without personal hygiene –
No washing, cleaning up, no hairpin in your hair,
Even the book you read last night is still left there,
Open on the bed. At the front of your house, the stream
Runs murmuring. You lie in the glade in a dream,
On open ground among the woods. Green mosses
Grow upon the rocks, under pine trees. Wind tosses
The soft slender grasses about, disturbing fly and bee.
Through the window, the birds are twittering so lazily.
Even the stone tiger that you put by the stairs looks kindly.
Oh my brother, you have reached a state that keeps identity
Of both object and self. When I look at myself, I must feel
My cognition has become so superficial, lacking in appeal.
I face your behaviour: suddenly see, if by you I could be taught,
I would have no worry from the world's most distracting thought.

(2)
Oh my brother, you are wealthy in erudition,
Still keeping on reading and living in seclusion.
You study calligraphy and your skill now exceeds
Zhang Xu, a great calligrapher, whose ink never bleeds.
You write poetry much better than Sima Xiangru,
The well-known writer of the famous chant, "Zixu fu."
You live in seclusion between the mountains two:
Mount Shi West and also Mount Shi East.
And you've lived there for ten years, at least.
You are strolling as if a wild man wandering.
Sometimes you follow the fisherman fishing.
Even though in autumn the wind is soughing
Through the tall but sparsely-leaved trees of wicker,
You would rather leave the world and choose here,
To be close, nearby my house across the river.

We're hand in hand together, we all are getting old
And your promises you keep, and keep like gold.

(3)
You hunt, to trap the foxy hare,
And fish and troll those underwater.
That is to satisfy your hunger,
Not for seclusion, keeping safer.
As for my life, I prefer to be quiet,
And eat a mostly-vegetarian diet.
However, for your lifestyle: you don't pick one –
Vegetarian or meat lover, as if a vessel-rich person.
I live by the Mountain of Zhongnan,
Wake up and sleep, a self-sufficient man,
Spending my life. But you spend a life so admirable –
The birds you meet, even – they don't escape your table.
Even wild animals enjoy being close to you.
The clouds and glow become your partners, too,
Accompanying you to kiss your robes and when
You turn your head, your hood cap and your face.
I think you enjoy your life, like Gu Kou Zhen,
Why do you still invite me to this reclusive place?

(1) Dong *Shan:* the name of a retreat for hermits. In the East Jin Dynasty, Xie An resigned from his official job and lived in seclusion on Mt. Dong at Hui Ji County in Zhejiang Province, and later returned to his society and made a great success. His story became an idiom for someone who has one life of failure and then another, very successful life later on.

(2) *Zhang Xu:* a calligrapher who lived in the Tang Dynasty. He also liked to drink. His cursive script affected the later calligraphers such as Huai Su and Yan Zhenqing.

(2) *Sima Xiangru:* a very famous writer, who wrote a many Fu – a special classical Chinese essay. Among them, the Fu "Zi Xu Fu" is very famous. But when he became old the Emperor only gave him a minor official position: guarding the graveyard of the Han Emperors.

(3) *vessel-rich person*: a person who spends their life in gorgeous luxury. In ancient times, people used vessels to eat, and a rich family would line up many vessels when they ate dinner.

(3 *Mountain Zhongnan*: it belongs to the same range as Mt. Qinling. It is located south of Xi'an City in Shanxi Province.

(3) *Gu Kou Zhen:* an idiom from the *Book of Han*. The story of the idiom is that Zheng Pu (Zheng Zizhen) lived in Gu Kou (Inner Valley) and concentrated on the great way (Taoism). Even when the great general Wang Feng gave him the valuable gift of hiring him, he refused to leave his meditation. Later, this idiom became an example of the hermit.

77. Zhang Wu Returns to Secluded Life

When I send you off and say goodbye,
I feel very disconsolate, as if I could cry.
A few days ago, we walked on hand in hand,
Now you're becoming a hermit – earlier than I.
You will go to the thatched-roof retreat
At the secluded Mountain of the East –
I wish I could…even sweep your wooden door…
I feel I should resign my official position, or…
How could you truly, actually do
Exactly what I would wish to do?

78. Waiting for Mr. Chu Guangxi's Visit *(But He Didn't Come)*

From the morning I have been waiting for you
By the door, and have kept opening the door, to
Pick up my ears to listen for the sounds of a cart.
I even jumped up to meet you, and with a start,
Many times, as if I heard the jade pendant dinging, dinging.
Now the clock that comes from Shangyuan is ringing –
It's time for twilight.
I don't know why the drizzle comes, against my wish.
Today you won't be here – now I understand fully,
(You have found no time to come to be with me).
However, I am still expecting to you come – it's mawkish.

Chu Guangxi: a friend of Wang Wei's, also a famous practitioner of pastoral landscape poetry.

Shangyuan: the Royal garden.

79. My Message to Governor Wei Zhi

I tell you the border town has become waste, stagnancy,
My eyes search anywhere: only the land wavering, empty.
In autumn the sky seems higher, but the sun seems different
From other places – it's too lonely. The wild geese lament
Going home, their voices sounding mournful, as if in sadness.
Upon the cold pool water lie reflections of the withered grass.
Outside of the hostel is the phoenix tree,
All over the ground have fallen its leaves…
Facing the end of the year, watching this scenery,
I only can feel to sing "Missing The Sad Elderly."
I couldn't make welcome an old friend, not for anything,
And so I spend this lonely life here in eastern Pingling.

Wei Zhi: a friend of Wang Wei, also a poet who created antiphonal poetry with Wang Wei.

Missing The Sad Elderly: an ancient melody of China.

Pingling: a place is in Xiangyang, Hubei Province.

80. Visiting the Hermit Cui Xingzong, with Lu Xiang

Here's the garden by your house and bower –
The leafy branch covers off your neighbour.
The green moss is very thick, and hides the dirt
Beneath the tall pine tree where you sit, inert,
And sprawl your long legs, lank hair thoroughly disheveled,
Rolling your eyes superciliously at how the world is peopled.

Cui Xingzong: Wang Wei's cousin. Before he became an officer, he lived a hermit's life.

Lu Xiang: a friend of Wang Wei's, also a poet in the Tang Dynasty.

Rolling your eyes: an idiom from Ruan Ji, a very famous poet, writer, and sage in the Wei and Jing Period. He had the ability to roll his eyes back to show only the whites. When his mother died, and his friend Ji Kang came by to console with him, he showed him the black eyes to welcome him. However, when Ji Kang's brother came, he showed the white eyes to express his dislike for him. Later, people used this idiom to express scorning somebody.

81. For My Cousin Wang Qiu, a Vice Director of Armament

When I was a teen, I rarely understood the world's affairs.
I studied very hard to attract fame and gain my full share.
I heard if I became an officer, a life of wealth I'd spend,
But suffered from the lack of talent to achieve this end.
Engaged in an official career path, I haven't ever really tried
To avoid the empty talk, to build up my contribution, to rise.
Since I am so helpless, I'd rather, along with my personality,
Resign from life, but I'm afraid of meeting some adversity.
Now it's cold, clear winter I can see the mountains far away,
Under deep snow – so thick, the woods appear a coacervate.
I really want to leave Dong Lin, retire; I'm inspired to pursue it,
And realize my wish to escape the world (and become a hermit).
Oh brother, like Huilian, an aloof stance you as well inherit –
In your early years you said you, like me, expected to keep away
From mundane affairs, but we go into the world to this very day.
We both wish to extend the date that we renounce together…
But the wings of time fly fast; we can't afford to wait forever.

Vice director of armament: an officer in charge of editing the books at the library.

Dong Lin: an official state position.

Spur the horse: pass the state examinations and attain a life of wealth.

Huilian: refers to Xie Huilian, Xie Lingyun's younger brother in the Southern Dynasty. He was very talented. Later, he became an example of a respectable younger brother with a good name.

82. For the Emperor's Poem Contest, *"Watching the Spring Scenery in the Rain from Penglai Palace to Xingqing"*

The Wei River zigzags, running, surrounding Qin Pass,
Mount Huang Lu hugs the palace environs, year by year.
Along the road rich in willows the imperial carriage steers.
The doors of the palace open one by one, from first to last –
Glancing back, the flowers have filled in the imperial garden.
Upon the most majestic clouds stands the palace's pavilions:
Spring rain greens the trees hide so many thousand households
The Emperor is on a tour here, respected by young and old.
I know it's to confirm the spring season, adjusting the role
Of heaven, not just for watching beautiful scenery unfold.

Penglai Palace (or Daming Palace): the one of three famous palaces in the Tang Dynasty, and the biggest one, located in present Longshou Yuan (Dragon Head Hill) in Xi'an, Shaanxi Province.

Xingqing Palace: the political centre during the reign of the Tang Emperor Xuanzong (Li Longji) between 712 and 755. It's one of the three largest palaces of the Tang Dynasty. The palace major Xuanzong and his concubine lady Yang lived in this palace. The famous poem, "The Song of Great Regret," described this palace. This poem was written by Bai Juyi, another Tang Dynasty poet.

Wei River: the biggest tributary of the Yellow River, located in the centre of Shaanxi Province.

Qin Pass: a suburb of Chang An in ancient China.

Mt. Huang Lu: presently in the northern part of Xingping County in Shaanxi Province.

83. Official Liu Is Sent to Anxi

To Yangguan you'll go, a border far away. Oh my friend,
A desert fills in the many nations, frontier dirt without end.
Now it's middle spring, though different from the mainland.
Occasionally you can see wild geese, but to find pedestrians,
Even if you go walking over the 10,000 miles, is very rare.
I hope you arrive safely and contribute to the royal culture,
Like bringing not only the Tian Ma – like General Li Guangli –
But also the alfalfa to feed them, to the mighty Han Emperor.
Or, like the imperial envoy bringing grapes to the Han Dynasty,
Fostering exchange between central plains and western border.
If you'd do something with the barbarians, let your power impress,
So they no longer have the nerve to ask for marriage with a
princess.

Officer Liu: he is the supervisor of the whole royal division and the monitor of all the officers and commoners in the palace and the palace grounds.

Tian Ma: the Ferghana horse of central Asia.

General Li Guangli: See footnote for poem 60.

Central plains: Zhongtu, Zhongzhou, or Huaxia. It indicates the core of Luoyang and includes the lower and middle reaches of the Yellow River. It's a cradle of Huaxia civilization.

western border: the region west of Yumen Pass and Yangguan Pass in the Han Dynasty. In the Tang Dynasty, the western border was extended to reach Burma and Persia; and in the Yuan Dynasty, the western border extended to Russia and even Africa.

84. To Pei Shidi

A beautiful landscape, and the setting sun, too –
A good time…to write poetry. I will invite you:
We'll watch together the remote sky, calm and meek,
Using the Ru Yi to prop up the pensive poet cheek.
The spring wind blows through the plants and grasses,
Vanillas bloom in my fence and as their fragrance passes,
The dim sunlight shines upon my house, fully, warmly;
The farmers drop round (or neighbours come visit me).
Spring is coming, all the trees and grasses growing up,
And the milt water pouring to the pool, as milk to cup.
Even though the plum and peach have not bloomed yet,
The full buds are covering their branches, all ready, set.
Please gather the sticks, the tools, to weed and prune–
I make bold to you: cultivation time comes very soon.

Ru Yi: back scratchers.

85. Goodbye to Officer Li Xin, on the High Hill

We say our goodbye on the top of a high hill.
The fields and river dale look so far and still,
Our gazes reaching towards the edges of the sky…

Then you have left…but still standing here am I.
At dusk the birds to their nests start to fly back,
And of your figure gradually, finally, I lose track.

Officer Li Xin: a Friend of Wang Wei's. He was in charge of personnel and selected advisors to the Emperor.

86. Enjoying the Village

(1)
I'm tired of always running into so many great palaces,
And passing by the numerous fine houses of marquises.
The official places of talented men who are dignitaries
Distinguish their backgrounds, and their social catches,
However, what is a man who lives in Mt. Kongdong caves,
With disheveled hair – when no one know how he behaves?

(2)
Even though again being conferred a noble rank
And a couple of white jades and the many thanks,
These can't compare with Nan Mu, cultivating my fields,
And sleeping in my Dongchuang – the joy this yields!

(3)
By the ferry, people picked up water chestnuts in the huge wind;
I walked with a cane, sunset bathing the west woods, and grinned.
The fishermen are fishing near the tree platforms of apricot,
The farmhouses sit there and about the peach orchard plot.

(4)
It's time for spring – the soft green grasses grow up anywhere,
And over by the village, pine trees reach tall in the summer air,
Their colours looking cool. It's getting dark, the cattle and sheep
All return by themselves, as if their shepherd boys could not keep
Up. And curiously, the following kids don't know me when
They see my official dress, insufficient in this certain acumen.

(5)
Under the mountain, the far-away village raises just a single smoke.
Beyond the high hill, a tree on the horizon stands, abides, uprightly.
I live in a bunkhouse, but have some good neighbours, like Yan
Hui,
And the opposite – like Mr. Wu Liu, who ancient sages does evoke.

(6)
Now is the lovely peach flower's blooming;
Its petals dripping the last night's raindrops.
After the rain, wickers their green assuming,
Spring's bodies are running – it never stops.
Through the misty morning, the petals fall –
Servant boys haven't yet started sweeping.
Orioles are twittering but the men who all
Live in the mountain (like me) keep sleeping.

(7)
When I drink, I just want to encounter a stream,
Then I'm getting drunk, then drink's supreme…
I like holding up, bracing, walls of tiles and leaning on
The huge, tall pine tree. In the morning, to "Nan Yuan"
(The garden in the south) I go, to pick up water-shields.
In evening, I come to "Dong Gu" (the east valley's fields)
To pound the yellow millet.

(1) Mt. Kongdong: a Taoist mountain located in Ping Liang City in Gansu Province, a good place for hermits.

(2) Nan Mu: the word comes from Tao Yuanming's poem, meaning a place for hermits to retreat.

(2) Dongchuang: master living room.

(5) Yan Hui: A foremost disciple of Confucius. He followed Confucius from the age of 14 until Confucius' death. Confucius always praised him. He had the reputation of being learned and kindhearted.

(5) Mr. Wu Liu: refers to Tao Yuanming (Jin Dynasty), who planted five willow trees by his house. So later, people called him Mr. Wu Liu, which means Mr. Five Willow Trees.

(7) Nan Yuan and Dong Gu: locations on the Wang River that Wang Wei used for seclusion.

87. To Officer Liu Lantian

The dog now rushes out, barking! Usually, it lies prone…
The lady is out of their poor house, her husband in a fright.
At the end of the year, he goes to pay his taxes downtown,
And comes back to his mountain village only at midnight.
After paying their money to the government, they only retain
A few defective fabrics and, by late harvest, but little grain.

Face this situation as a man and as an officer –
How can you say you "have nothing you can do"?
Please concern yourself about their suffering, sir.

88. Mr. Yan and Another Friend Visit My House in Late Spring

Pines and chrysanthemums fill in about,
And even hide, the three paths to my house.
I spend my hermit life with five-carts books.
Welcome to you – come, and I will cook
The okra for you, my honoured guests.
You can enjoy the bamboo and the rest
Of the plants growing about my poor house.
Time flies so fast, spring grass just sprouts,
And birds–magpies–are feeding their babies…
In a moment, flowers are all fading, unease
Finding the orioles, now twittering with sadness.
Though I'm surely getting old, and could confess
My hair's so grey, it's almost turning yellow,
I will reduplicate the time, reading more now,
And enjoying the beautiful sights,
As I've done before, and ready life.

three paths: refers to a story from the New Dynasty (established by Wang Mang, who usurped power between the East Han and West Han Dynasties). Officer Jiang Yi didn't care to follow Wang Mang. He resigned and dug three paths in his courtyard to show that he only wanted to see Qiu Zhong and Yang Zhong, making one path for him and two others for his good friends. Later, three paths symbolized people who resign and go back home to spend life as a hermit.

five-carts: refers to many books. This idiom is from the book, *Zhuangzi.*

89. Sitting Alone on an Autumn Night

Sitting alone, my grey hairs causing me some sorrow,
In my midnight living room, awaiting a tomorrow,
I hear the fruit of the mountain orchard falling in the rain,
And under the light, some insects chirping, off and on again.
I understand my once-black, thick hair can't return to me…
It's impossible: longevity, through any known gold alchemy.
As well, I understand, and have to say,
If I want to remove the illness and decay,
The unique way to learn Wu Sheng: non-birth, non-death:
It is to recurrently learn to walk the Buddha's sunlit path.

gold alchemy: a story that comes from the history book, *Shi Ji*. Emperor Wu of the Han Dynasty was visited by the necromancer Luan Da, who said that he could find the most precious herb of immortality. He claimed he could cut gold with his hand and make this herb. The Emperor was very happy and gave him a senior position. But eventually, the Emperor found there was no effect from this herb. Then the Emperor killed him.

Wu Sheng: non-birth, non-death. It's also call Nirvana.

90. After Saying Goodbye to My Brother Jin and Climbing to the Qinglong Temple to Watch Mount Lantian

I just said goodbye to you at the ridge, my younger brother Jin…
Now I'm standing here, looking down at the farthest suburban
Areas – at Qinglong temple, it's all darker and gloomier.
I climb the high hill, but I cannot see any known features,
Except the mountains and clouds, nature's plain face.
From far away the huge trees hide the traveler's trace
And the sky covers the castle completely, roof to base.
I am worried about you playing your official part…
And don't know where I can find your official cart…

Jin: Wang Jin, Wang Wei's younger brother, who helped General Li Guang Bi crack down on the rebellion of An and Shi. He then became a prime minister. After the rebellion was over, owing to his brother Wang Wei capitulating to An and Shi and becoming an official of their government, he had to save his brother's life. Wang Wei was arrested and being punished, but Wang Jin reported to the Emperor, offering to resign his official position and substitute himself for Wang Wei's offence. Finally, not only did he save his brother's life, but also helped his brother recover an official position. He was also a poet and had remarkable skill at calligraphy. Like his brother, he was also a Buddhist, and encouraged the government to support Buddhism and build many temples.

91. In a Winter Night's Snowstorm, Recalling Lay-Buddhist Mr. Hu's House

In the dusk I heard the sound of the night watch,
In the morning, face to the mirror, I find a batch –
All over that face – of age-speckles showing.
Outside the window the wind was blowing
Through the bamboo. I open the icy door –
The snow's covered up the entire mountain.
It's drifting down from the sky's quiet core
And deeply filling in the lane, and later, when
All the fields are covered by snow, it seems empty
And leads my heart along to drifting leisurely.
Suddenly I recall you, my friend – very similar
To the legendary man Yuan An you are, inflexible.
How's it going for you? Do you close your door,
Live a poor life, rejecting the friend-remedy, still?

Yuan An: a great officer in the East Han Dynasty. One year, the city had a great snowstorm, and all the poor people went out to sweep snow from doorways and to beg. Only Yuan An's house was still buried under the snow, the door kept closed. The country magistrate thought he'd died and asked the workers to force open his door. They discovered him lying on the bed. They asked him why he did not go out to sweep the snow and get money to buy some food. He said, "I won't bother others, as too many people go out to beg."

92. Visiting Zen Master Fu’s Temple

A path twists through to the mountain valleys.
The master’s temple’s hidden among the trees
And among the clouds.There’s the wall painting,
Of the immortal whose musical wings are playing,
And a fairy maiden bending down upon her knees,
To burn incense from the bamboo garden,
The sunshine bathing the whole mountain.
It looks very splendid, the stream covered by cirrus –
It looks very cool and so clear. But are you curious
About how long the master does sitting meditation?
Make of this spring fragrance holder some observation…

Spring fragrance holder: the master – when he did sitting meditation for a long time and then emerged to go walking, his spirit, with no more worry or anxiety in his heart, carried a spring fragrance.

93. In Spring – the Pattern of a Master's Life

He likes reading the eminent monk's biography,
Acquiring the knowhow to stop dieting entirely,
By practicing Qi Gong (how to keep fit lifelong).
He's about 80 or 90 years old, and walking along
With his cane – patterns of turtledoves about it thread.
And he does use a turtle shell as the foot of his bed.
Out of his window the green wicker trees reflect
The mountain's own green. At dusk one may detect
The nesting birds, hiding within the pear tree woods,
Being so quiet there, under their crests, caps and hoods.
By the north window, under the peach and plum tree,
He burns incense, does sitting meditation, leisurely.

patterns of turtledoves: in the Han Dynasty, the Emperor gave elderly people who were around 80 or 90 years old a special gift representing longevity: a jade cane with a turtledove pattern. As turtledoves never suffer from choking, they are another symbol of longevity.

use a turtle shell as the foot of his bed: According to the "Shi Ji" record, once in Southern China an old man used a turtle as the foot of his bed. After over 20 years, the old man died but the turtle was still alive. It's also a symbol of longevity.

94. Sending Off Shen Zifu, to Jiangdong

At Yangliu Ferry, it's an absence of guests.
The fishermen pulling the boat take rests.
You, my friend, have departed, to Linqi…
Let my yearning keep following behind you
Like the spreading optimal spring river view,
From the southern to the northern Yangtze.

Shen Zifu: a friend of Wang Wei's. The date of his birth and death and his life story are unknown.

Jiangdong: an eastern branch of the Yangtze River, presently near Nanjing City in Jiangsu Province.

Linqi: a land close to the shore, here indicating the eastern shore of the Yangtze River.

95. A Villa at Mount Zhongnan

After middle age, I prefer Buddhism, then
After becoming elderly, I find Mt. Zhongnan.
Every time there when I want fun,
I wish to go outside my villa alone,
The happiness only enjoyable by one –
I walk along the river until the terminus of the river should come,
Then I'm sitting there to watch the clouds build up and down.
Occasionally, I encounter an old man who's living near around.
If we're chatting or laughing, I even forget the time I'm to go home.

Mt. Zhongnan: also see the footnote of poem 61.

96. Mount Zhongnan

The summit of Mt. Taiyi supports the sky,
Even reaching up to the palace of heaven,
Connecting the seashore to the mountain.
Looking back, I see the white clouds lie,
Lingering and combining together.
At first it's misty but when I enter
Inside, I can see nothing, wherever I scan.
The middle of the summit of Mt. Zhongnan
Is divided south and north into two parts, and they
Are totally different – the cloudy and the sunny day.
I want to cross the river to stay in a lodge, so I ask
The woodcutter whether he's available for this task.

Taiyi: please see the footnote of poem 61.

Mt. Zhongnan: also see the footnote of poem 61.

97. For Pei Di, at the Wang River, in Leisure

The mountain in autumn turns cold, then colder
But as well seems to grow out greener, fresher,
And the water runs slowly down to the shore.
I stand with my cane in the old wooden door,
Looking out, hearing Fall cicada sounds near me.
The setting sun is shining down upon the ferry;
From the village rises cooking smoke, sparsely.
Again I meet you, drunk, over-watered like Jie Yu –
You sing jubilantly, a man like Tao Yuanming, too.

Jie Yu: A talented person who lived in Chu in the Spring and Autumn period, who did not wish to become an official and so pretended to be mad. He usually cultivated farmland to support himself and his family. Later, he and his wife moved to Mt. E Mei to do meditation. They all became famous Taoist immortals (for over 2000 years now).

Mr. Wu Liu: Please see the footnote of poem 86.

98. Farmers

The old grain stores are almost over, eaten, uninsured,
And the fresh wheat seedlings haven't yet matured.
People are getting old but stint on their porridge, eat less –
Though they're elders, it's shabby how they have to dress.
The sparrow's brown breast bobs, feeding its nestlings
In the green moss by the well in sudden starts.
The cocks crow by the chipped door needing painting.
The skinny cows pull the poor, ramshackle carts.
The cowboy wearing slight straw sandals grazes
Not cattle, but strong pigs who can best survive.
Massive rains tear down the red pomegranates,
But autumn taros' rich green leaves now thrive.
At noon the farmers take a rest under the mulberry;
They won't be returning home till shadows are long.
They call their whereabouts Foolish Old Man Valley,
How can the tax man (I) question their right and wrong?

Foolish Old Man Valley: a place located in Zibo City in Shandong Province. Once in the state of Qi, the King of Huan gathered a hunting party. The deer they were chasing escaped into a valley where they subsequently encountered an old man who told them that the valley was called Foolish Old Man Valley. The King wondered if this particular old man could be the foolish old man. The old man said when some time before, when his cow gave birth to a calf, he was waiting for the calf to grow up as he wanted to sell it to buy a horse. A young man heard this and came to the old man's house and took the calf away, saying, "a cow never gives birth to a horse." His neighbours heard this news and they all laughed at him. And so the name Foolish Old Man Valley came to be created.

99. Leisurely Living on the Wang River

Once, *if,* I return to white community, hermit style,
I'll never again think of green gate, the official.
Leaning on the old tree under my eaves, I'll
Observe how rural village times may go –
By the water field, wild rice shoots grow;
White birds in flocks fly over the mountain.
Like Chen Zhongzi in Yuling, I live here,
Hoisting (using the Ju Gao, a simple lever)
Well water to sprinkle my vegetable garden.

white community: the idiom comes from the Jin Dynasty. A man called Dong Chong established a white community (meaning a renunciate community) and did meditation. Later this referred to a hermit life.

green gate: in the Tang Dynasty, this refers to the east gate of Chang An where all the official fields are.

Chen Zhong Zi: an ideologist hermit in Qi State, he strove to spend a poor but clear life. He tired of his brother's rich life so he separated from him, and went to live in Ling Zi. He used the Ju Gao to take water from wells and pour it over other people's gardens. Eventually he died of starvation.

Ju Gao: a simple watering tool to carry water from wells, very similar to a lever. It was created in the Spring and Autumn period.

100. Thanks, Zhang Yin

My friend Zhang Yin is much skilled in calligraphy,
In painting, fortune-telling and in poetry,
And recently has written a fine poem for me –
So now this poem for him I'm writing, gratefully.

You never follow the road to that
City of the East Ranger; not like he
Sitting back so idly in the usual hat,
On cushions, to play the Tan Zi, ready.
Like Shu Zhong's old man, Yan Junping,
You could set up a shop for fortune-telling.
In the manner of a Luoyang scholar,
You recite in a voice deep and strong
Your poetry, and the herbs and flowers
About your cottage thrive and throng.
On the front desk where you often lean,
You play the lute like Huizi, very keen.
Your highlight skill, though, is in painting –
You paint a screen like famous Cao Bo'xing,
Who when he spilled ink once, O! the horror
Even distracted Sun Quan, who's the Emperor.
Your cursive script outstrips Nei-Shi-Wang
Xizhi's fan calligraphy. It is that strong.
Your hermit life, in your hometown,
Without any worries, year after year,
Has you pulling your curtains down –
Reading and writing you hold very dear.
The walk to your neighbours is fairly long,
And you like to think you're like Cai Yong.
You are getting older, and older anew –
So, who should I give these books to?

Zhang Yin: a poet, painter, and calligrapher, the fifth younger male cousin of Wang Wei. When he was young, he and Wang Wei shared a hermit life on Mt. Shao Shi for about 10 years, then went out and became officers. Later, Zhang Yin resigned and returned to his hometown where he lived out the remainder of his life.

City of the East Ranger: a place of much unemployment and idleness, full of street urchins, though wealthy.

Tan Zi: an ancient board game. It can be played alone.

Yan Junping: a famous fortune-teller in Shu (Sichuan Province). A very famous Taoist in the later West Han Dynasty. He could predict the future. He predicted two things 20 years before they happened. One was that Wang Mang would usurp power and establish a New Dynasty, the other was that Emperor Guang Wu would destroy Wang Mang's power and recover East Han (reconstituting the Han Dynasty).

Huizi: also called Hui Shi, born in Song State in the Warring States period. He was trained in the school of logicians. He made a friend in Zhuang Zi. He liked sitting under the phoenix tree, playing the lute. When he felt tired, he would lean on the tree to take a nap.

Cao Bo'xing: a famous painter in the Three Kingdoms period, who drew a portrait of the Emperor Sun Quan, which people actually thought not a painting, but somehow real.

Sun Quan: An Emperor of Wu State in the Three Kingdoms period.

Nei-Shi-Wang Xizhi: a famous calligrapher in the East Jin Dynasty. A story about Wang Xizhi has him helping an old lady to sell her fans. It tells how he met her selling her fans at Mount Gan and wrote five words on her fans – and then how all the people scrambled to buy them.

Cai Yong: a very famous writer, calligrapher, and philosopher in the East Han Dynasty. As well, the very famous father of the talented lady Cai Yan. He liked collecting books and had over 10,000, but after he died in jail, only 4,000 books remained. Most of these books he had given to others as gifts. He was a knowledgeable, brilliant man of the East Han Dynasty.

101. To an Officer from Wu

My friend comes from northern Wu to the southern capital as an officer of the state, but he's unaccustomed to Chang An's summer heat. And so I send to him this poem.

You're sent from the south to the Capital as an officer,
But you're unaccustomed to Chang An's heat in summer.
In your guest house it is boiling, horrid.
It's hard relieving heat without tea porridge!
It's useless waving a fan around to relieve
The bitterness of a homesick summer, I believe,
As life, merely by itself, is suffering's root and cause.
Your hometown's light blue silk bags have no flaws
But carrying one around with you just makes you sigh
For the hometown pickled mackerels (not yet arrived).
The local boiled pancakes . . . how can one *eat* here?
For me, though, it's better to choose a life that's freer:
Go back to my hometown, wear the light grass slipper,
Catch the fish along the shore of ancient Fuchun River.

suffering's root: (Dukkha) a word invented by the Buddha, meaning unsatisfactory. According to his teaching, root (significance) means the true is true. Buddha said the inherited quality of all the things in the world is Dukkha.

Fuchun River: located in Zhejiang Province. A story was spread there about a famous hermit, Yan Ziling, who lived and fished there, enjoying life on the Fuchun. He had been a classmate of Liu Xiu, and when Liu Xiu became the Emperor Guan Wu, he invited Yan Zi Ling several times to become a senior officer. But Yan Zi Ling refused, preferring to live by the Fuchun River until he passed way. Right away, his fishing stage became a tourist attraction.

102. Going to Baxia at Dawn

I go to late spring Ba Gorge at dawn.
It recalls the capital, Chang An.
The sky's there, and the rivers run,
And a washer girl washing clothing,
All bathing in the over-rising sun,
And all the local cocks are crowing…

There are fishier remote fishing villages,
Just getting along, doing boat business,
But all in all and in the main, they're fine.
The mountain bridge lies above the tree line.

When I'm climbing the high mountain,
All the villages rising before my eyes,
Far into the distance, I can see and scan
Clearly the two main Yangtze tributaries.
As a human I've learnt the ascent of choice,
But the oriole still keeps his original voice.
It's fortunate I understand mountain/river happiness –
That can a little bit relieve my feeling of homesickness.

Ba Gorge (Baxia): refers to one of the Three Gorges of the Yangtze River, in the section from Ba County to Pu Ling County. This was the location of the ancient country "Ba". Its culture is still a mystery.

the two main Yangtze tributaries: refers to the Lang and Bai rivers located in Sichuan Province.

103. Sitting Alone, Missing My Cousin Cui Xingzong, this Autumn Night

It’s a night so quiet all
The animals and insects have stopped moving,
Only the cicadas’ call
Still lingers in my ears, softly clear and ringing.

In my courtyard the tall pagoda trees are found,
Blowing in the north wind, sighing their sounds.
The setting sun in early autumn's early down.
I miss you – the letters we sent I kept around.

I know that now you have become an officer
And my life will be being another retired elder.
At the end of my life period, I miss the place, Cangzhou,
And though the talented person doing official work is you,
This is changeable, morning or night, on command…
Would you like to come with me, return to the farmland?

Cangzhou: a shoreside place where hermits live.

104. I Sight Grey Hair

How can my age become so old so fast?
My hair gets greyer, and greyer day by day.
Between heaven and earth, life's a flash –
How long can this passer-through yet stay?
Disconsolate, the cloud of my hometown mountain
Hesitates, and dreams away, facing the setting sun.
What sort of things can I even consider to begin
To speak of to the present people I don't know.
From east castle to south path, on my walk I go.

105. A Poem for the Present Spring Garden

It's rain last night, the fields are wet,
Farmers their wooden sandals get;
It's time for cold spring, the year resets.
They put on their poor cotton jackets;
They dig the ridged field, water down the ribbing field,
Red peach flowers bloom among trees of green wicker;
At the break, they draw a chessboard; to chess they yield.
On the other side of the trees, works the Ju Gao leaver;
Then at dusk someone brings a small deerskin table
To lean on, to shelter their bodies in the grass, as able.

Ju Gao: the water pump described in footnote of poem 99.

106. Passing by He Sui's Medicine Garden in Spring

A couple of years ago you had a hibiscus fence,
Now it's gone, yet this does still make sense –
Fresh medical racks have been set up instead…
Herbs like Mr. Vanilla, a fine gentleman, well fed.
Famous ones!! Like Chang Qing (Sima Xiangru)!!
The stream pours over circular stone, you see clear through,
Canes stake the old pine; it seems to be growing up well, too.
When you meet a painter merely passing by, you bow, though;
You rush to meet him, putting each shoe toes in heel, heel in toe.
When cooking zizania rice, you're sure to use sugarcane syrup,
And try to find wolf berries for your Malabar Nightshade Soup.
You understand how to grow the herbal garden very well,
And like Chen Zhongzi of Yuling, never indulge yourself.

Zizania rice: wild rice. The old time monks often ate this.

Chang Qing (Sima Xiangru): a writer – please see footnote of poem 76.

Chen Zhongzi or Yuling: an ideologist hermit – please see footnote of poem 99.

putting each shoe toes in heel, heel in toe: a Chinese idiom that means warmly welcoming someone's visit and eagerly treating someone in a very friendly and hospitable manner. The idiom comes from Ruan Ji's Story: one day Ruan Ji had a party at home. He heard that Wang Can was coming and rushed out to meet Wang, even wearing his shoes backwards (with Chinese shoes, it's possible). The guests wondered why he rushed out to meet the guest like that, and even let Wang sit in a top seat, respectfully recommending Wang to his guests.

107. A Lodging in a Buddhist Monk's Temple

A Buddhist master lives on Mount Taibai –
From the summit, his smoke is rising high.
Over the valleys, his lively Buddhist music will run,
His Buddhist flowers like rain fall on the mountain.
His trance is hidden deep beyond any heart-emotion,
But his name is spared over, as Buddha he has shown.
When the birds are migrating, he just watches birds.
When visitors depart, he meditates without words.
In the morning, I walk to the end of the pine trail;
In the evening, I bed down inside this very temple.
In the cave house hidden well within deep bamboo woods,
At night, from far away the stream's sound softly spreads.
Before, this would have been like clouds or dew or dreams
But, right now here on my pillow, this is reality, it seems.
And look: this lodge, this peace, is not just temporary:
Serving Buddha – this, my whole life will accompany.

Mount Taibai: located among the Mei, Taibai, and Zhouzhi counties. It's a watershed between the Fen and Wei rivers. It's the highest mountain in Shaanxi Province.

108. Staying With Officer Wei on the Mountain

It's very lucky you chose me,
That I have an opportunity
To come away with you and go
Out of the noisy, worldly show.

From this mountain nest I now see
Flowers colour-in the rocky valley,
And the fir or pine trees all reflect within
The clear steam journeying down-mountain.
Suddenly, the birds are twittering by the creek
And the clouds come round as if to hug the peak.

The people touring here are all Zan Fu level officers,
Attended by palace musicians and imperial censors
Like Kui Long. What if I refuse to visit the official rote
But still hear the state clock's surrounding notes?
This morning I go to meet you as the officer –
How can I not hurry with my cart, oh sir?

Zan Fu: ancient superior officer's head wear with a special hair pin and an official seal.

Kui Long: it is said that in the Shun period they had two ministers: one was the Kui, the musical officer; the other was the Long, the censor. Later, people took this example to mean officers of high position.

109. A Hanshi Festival Moment at the East Of the Castle

Through the peach and plum woods rustling,
By the water's shoreline, something's drifting
As green cattails nod, angelica root moistening.
Along its course, a few households are spotted,
The languid stream with fallen flowers dotted.
Younger people's soccer: it's so absurd:
They kick the ball over the flying bird;
They play on swings, with joy they cry,
Over the weeping poplars they try to fly!
Younger ones have fun, play without having any schedule –
Not needing to wait for the Qingming or Shangsi Festival.

Hanshi Festival: held every April 4th, commemorating the time of King Zhong Er of Jin State and his secretary, Jie Zhi Tui, who followed and cared for him, even when they were starving, cutting some meat from his own leg to feed Zhong Er. See footnote of poem 67.

Qingming: the Qingming Festival is one of 4 important festivals in China (the Spring [New Year] Festival, the Lantern Festival, the Qingming Festival, and the Mid-Autumn Festival) as well as one of the 24 Chinese seasonal divisions. After the Hanshi Festival, every year on April the 5th, the Han Nation and some minor nations celebrated this festival. They held great sacrificial ceremonies like tomb sweeping to remember their ancestors or take spring tours. This ongoing festival has a 4000-year history.

Shangsi Festival: also called the Girl Festival. In ancient China, every lunar year on the 3rd of March, people go to the riverside to bathe and pray for their bad luck to be removed. As well, there is the Peach Flower Festival, when girls become women and can marry. This festival could be called Chinese Valentine's Day. Nowadays in Japan they still have this festival, called Hina Matsuri, though right now on the Chinese mainland this festival is not popular. Some minor nations still keep very similar celebrations like The Water Sprinkling Festival of the Dai Nation (within China).

110. Red Peony

The new green leaves open, quietly and leisurely,
The colours dark and bright, of the lovely peony.
In time, its own fading it faces, heartbroken to be not.
Oh, Spring scenery, do you know the peony's thought?

111. Qiwu Qian Resigns and Returns Home

I've spent my time in an open-minded society,
But I haven't seen your kind of talent previously.
I would rather resign and be the same as you.
Fatality never complains, but human life, it's true,
Has lofty ideals and the surpassing will to be free –
I thought of you resigning, unhesitatingly –
Now you face your impoverishment quietly.

I imagine it's so clear in autumn, on your remote river
The setting sun scatters light across its empty water;
The long-drawn-out, cloudless night comes on and soon
You drive the boat along, approaching the bright moon…
Soft light shines upon the fish and bird life gathering;
Tranquilly, the long reed marsh your vessel's crossing.

Unnecessary to change, should a guest come out your way,
Even if your long grey hair hangs disheveled every day.
Like me, a stupid, lazy person ignorant of worldly noise,
Living in this simple place, far from the Emperor's voice,
Just another humble being, forgotten, that no one employs
But who is the fairest, and the ablest one, a charmer…
I follow you, returning to the field as an old farmer.

112. A Poem to Scholar Sun

You live right here in our great capital, Chang An –
Of course, the scenery, and life, are as they first began.
As well, you come from an imperial family like Jian Ping's.
You sleep on rich pillows, patterned bamboo and other things;
You eat the special melon "Wu Se" – it's imperial,
And furthermore, is served upon a gold plate, after all.
However, when you come over to visit me here
There is no coarse wine to offer you, or even deer –
We can only eat the "Hu Ma dinner" – a very similar meal
To those eaten under pine trees. (*Hermit like*, some may feel.)
Please do not hate the bitterness of farm lifestyle,
And extend your return date for a longer while.

Jian Ping: a prince of Song State of the Southern Dynasty. Hs father's name was Liu Hong; his son's name Liu Jingsu. They all enjoyed literature, were courteous to the wise and respectful to scholars. They wrote many books.

Wu Se Melon: means Five Colour Melon. Another name for it is the Dong Ling melon. In the early Han Dynasty, a man named Shao Ping used to be a Marquis in Dong Ling in the Qin Dynasty. After Qin disappeared, he assumed another role and became a melon farmer. His melons were extremely delicious; all the people were competing to buy them. They called it the Dong Ling melon or the Wu Se melon. Unfortunately, nowadays these melons have disappeared.

"Hu Ma dinner": a vegetarian meal with rice and sesame paste.

113. A Royal Guard's Wife

Over the high castle, the autumn moon is shining,
From the windows, the sound of music's spreading…
Causing the royal guard's wife's thoughts to start.
She is worrying about the dining hall, she is apart
From her husband so long now, and her little boy
Is playing by the footsteps with his simple toy.
Moonlight shines into the door, quiet is about–
She hears the horses' clip clop, and she rushes out,
Watching their bridles of blue silk, passing by…
They've almost gone, but to see her husband she doubts.
She looks around, they all say nothing, no one tries;
They watch each other with tears waiting in the eyes.

114. To the Spagyrist Who Lives on Mount Tai

You follow a calling going back years, over a thousand;
And you have lived at all the five famous mountains.
If I may, in your honour, list your illustrious abilities:
You know the Ding, the tripod altar from ancient Qi,
And you just passed by the cottage at Wangmu.
If you couldn't follow Confucius or Mo Tzu, being too free,
Which thing need you ask such hermits as Chang, Ju though?
You play jade wind music, and the phoenix comes to you,
And you use the bronze plate to fish the liquid blue.
To speak, you launch your body into the air like a spark
And your eyes are so bright you even write letters in the dark.
You have, of course, skill to turn on cinnabar & mercury,
And often talk about the initial heaven-and-earth's alchemy.
An imperial edict asking you to send a memorandum
On how to refine alchemy, from the Throne has come.
Your life receives respect from the high imperial court,
Like rush bags on wheels make a soft-wheel cart.
Your life on the mountain is so quiet, I even hear
The murmuring of distant streams clearer in my ear.
The pine trees themselves get so very high,
The branches become sparse and twisted, dry.
I clasp my face between my hands before a woodcutter.
"How about if I return to the world again?" I stutter.

Spagyrist: alchemist.

the Ding, the tripod altar from ancient Qi: in the Spring and Autumn period, the King of Qi expected to get an invaluable Tripod from the state of Lu, but the King of Lu took a substitute Tripod to offer him in order to subvert their peace agreement. But the King of Qi doubted its authenticity, and said: "I will believe this to be a counterfeit Tripod unless Liu Xia Hui (a man of faith from Lu State) tells me this is a real Tripod." So the King of Lu asked Liu to tell the King of Qi that the counterfeit Tripod was real, but Liu refused. Liu said, "If you think your Tripod is a national symbol, you don't want to give it to the King of Qi. But for me, the faith is much more important than the Tripod. I don't want to lie." Finally the King of Lu gave the King of Qi the real Tripod, and Qi and Lu made a peace agreement.

Wangmu: indicates a pool at Mt. Tai, which is the location of a legend, that in Yao Chi (Heaven) was a pool where the immortal Queen Mother of the West lived.

Mo Tzu (Mozi): a very famous philosopher, politician, scientist, militarist in the Spring and Autumn and Warring States periods. He established Mohism, which emphasized inoffensiveness and universal love. He wrote the book, *Mozi,* and he is a prominent representative of "The One Hundred" pre-Qin philosophers.

Chang, Ju: two hermits, one a tall hermit, the other a strong hermit – in Chu State in the Spring and Autumn Period. When Confucius and his disciples were travelling through all the kingdoms, they lost their way at one point. A disciple, Zi Lu, asked a tall person who was farming there the way, but the farmer didn't tell him. He instead encouraged Zi Lu to leave Confucius and follow him, and learn to cultivate!

s*oft wheel cart:* rush bags were bound to the wheels to more comfortably move around important people visiting court. It became an idiom for taking extra care to treat venerable persons well.

115. Farewell for Officer Mi

In the eastern suburbs the grasses turn Spring colours;
By horse you soon leave for the frontier. Furthermore,
Away from your hometown, there you hear apes crying,
And amid strangeness, watch the river Xiang running.
You will dedicate a monument to the Throne
For the inhabitants who live where you have gone.
You will await dignitaries at the inn by the river.
Local people you hire become varieties of Officer.
Elegant hostels you will visit, try to get you to entwine –
You'll be like a lonely oriole twittering in a remote shrine,
A wild apricot growing at the post house by the ravine.
Now I go to the palace to report to the Emperor
In the morning or evening, whenever I'm asked for;
But you stay out at Nanzhong this Autumn.
Attend the Jiqiu festival (here, a taboo custom).

Nanzhong: the southern part of Sichuan Province, and the entire areas of Yunnan, and Guizhou provinces.

Jiqiu Festival: another name for the Mid-Autumn Festival. During this Festival, there are many taboos. For example, men must never pray to the moon because the moon represents the female. A person who is physically disabled or very weak wouldn't pray to the moon, as legend says this would result in further disabilities and weaknesses.

116. Sending Off Xiong Jiu, Who's to Assume Office at Anyang

Wei Country's Ying / Liu, two venerable sages,
Lived in the time of the Three Kingdoms age.
It was so solitary – full of all the elegant empty.
The river Zhang, as in the old time, ran free,
But they will keep manners and clear morality.
The old Bronze Sparrow Terrace stands amid
Crisscross footpaths between fields. You'll like it.
And the Golden Tiger stands for the common man.
I'll send off your cart at the Ba River in Chang An
Out of Guangdong you will ride your horse.
We're at a distance of 1000 miles, of course,
But in the vegetable garden in the west (Xi Yuan),
We will have the same night, have the same moon.

Ying / Liu: one name for both Ying Yang and Liu Zhen, writers who lived in the time of The Three Kingdoms in the country of Wei. They were two of The Seven (seven sages living in the period of Jian An). They both had high writing skills (poetry, essays, and Fu).

Bronze Sparrow Terrace: a terrace built by Cao Cao, prime minister in Wei Country in the Three Kingdoms period. It's Cao Cao and his son's luxury retreat.

Golden Tiger: another terrace built at the same time as the Bronze Sparrow.

Guandong: the area east of the Shanhai Pass. Presently in the northeast region.

117. Showing My Younger Brother Something on the Mountain

I live in the jungle, gradually forgetting myself.
You attend an adult ceremony, become an adult.
Do not learn, like Ji Kang did, the trait of laziness;
But you should reconcile yourself, despite the stress,
To a life of poverty, like the great Yuan Xian.
You know the shaded side of hermit mountain.
It's facing the many windows to the distant north.
But at the eastern suburbs, the river goes forth.
Karma gathers together, and illusion gets all ready,
Though you don't have warm hearts, validity can let be...
How do you know Guan Cheng Zi's embodiment is not me?

Ji Kang: an ideologist, musician, and literati. One of the seven sages of the bamboo grove. He married Cao Cao's granddaughter, but he did not wish to become an officer. His laziness was very famous. He would take only one bath every two weeks and would laze in bed until he could hardly hold his urine.

Yuan Xian: an idiom that comes from the famous history, "Zhuang Zi." Yuan Xian was a disciple of Confucius. He was contented in poverty and devoted to things spiritual and refused to become an officer. He lived in a room with a grass door and used half a broken water jar as a window.

Guang Cheng Zi: a hermit or immortal who lived in the time of the Yellow Emperor. It was said he lived in a cave on Mt. Kongtong in Gansu Province. He is the first patriarch of Taoism.

118. A Visit to Huagan Temple

Here's a temple, Huagan Temple,
With fine jade incense-gathering sticks,
And underneath, flooring of glazed bricks.
There's two designs in the art of the mural:
One is many pavilions connecting
To the palace of the Dragon King.
The other one is the Tiger's Den,
Guarding the keep from the barbarian.
Its temple's in the valley, though it's very quiet.
By the door, stands the great green summit.
The only sound's the music of wind-blown pine;
The mountain is so deep, I haven't even heard
The intermittent twittering of the forest bird.
The darkness of the crevices gets a golden shine
As the sunlight dyes the woods through and through.
The path to the temple is totally different, too;
It's hiding amongst the tops of golden clouds.
And the River Qing may even have a rainy day
While on the slopes sun bathing the sun allows.
To offer fruit to the temple in their own way,
Wild geese fly and drop. And the deer even run
Along the flower path to leave where they are from
And convert their restless speed, to sleep here.
I enjoy the scenery of the mountain far and near.
By the surrounding fence grow wild vegetables;
Wild cherry trees find the empty hostel amenable.
We eat delicious meals cooked with the Hu rice,
And green asparagus sprouts up, also very nice.
I swear to follow the monk's sutra-reading voice,
And sit in meditation, learning how to keep my choice:
Infinity.

Huagan Temple: though an old Tang Dynasty temple often mentioned by poets, it no longer exists.

Infinity (Wu Sheng): no birth or death. It's known as Nirvana.

119. A Tour in Winter

I walk away out of the east gate of the castle,
And try to open my eyes to see far ahead when,
Beyond the boundless forests rises the mountain,
And shrinks the sun into the plain, its vassal.
River Wei runs to the north, through Handan City,
In the east the pass is out of Hangu, still.
The capital, at Qin, gathers many people
Who come from so many places, ugly and pretty,
And many provincial governors come to meet the Emperor, too.
Many officers are at Xianyang, strutting like crowing cocks,
Many officers and dignitaries chase each other, throwing rocks.
The prime minister (an old marquis) selects from the Lie Hou,
The nobles to give a farewell dinner to The Guang Lu
(An official position close to the Emperor).
However, a man after myself is Sima Xiangru,
He just gets old, finds an illness, gets sore –
He only can return to the lodge at Mao Ling, too.

Handan City: a capital of the State of Zhao in the Warring States period. An idiom comes from this city: a young man from the State of Yan visiting Zhao found that its people had very good posture when walking, and so he imitated them, but eventually not only did he not learn the Zhao's but also forgot the Yan's manner of walking and had to crawl back home!

Hangu Pass: one of eight famous passes in ancient China. It is located in Sanmen Xia City in Henan Province. The western area of this pass leans on the highland, and its east side ends at impassable steep creeks; the southern segment connects with Mt. Qin Ling, and its north borders on, nearly blocking up, the Yellow River. If one man is guarding the pass, ten thousand are unable to get through. It's a very important citadel.

Xianyang: the outskirts of Chang An, the capital city during the Tang Dynasty. A city where most officers would come to the capital to meet the Emperor. It is located in the western area of Xi'an City in Shaanxi Province.

Mao Ling: the tomb of the Emperor of Wu in the time of the Han Dynasty. It is the largest royal tomb from the Han era and is located on Wu Ling Hill between Xianyang City and Xingping City in Shaanxi Province.

120. A Poem for My Melon Garden

During leisure time I like to hoe around the melon,
And lean upon the useful hoe as if I'm listening to
Someone knocking on the door. And the distinguished few
Dignitaries ride their famous horses with their own
Servants, the attendants driving the dignitary's cart,
Passing by the remote lane full of the music of
The nearby imperial court. The old friends I know and love
Still live here with me. We stand together, yet apart.
We go chase the cool wind hand in hand, and rest our hearts,
To watch the world. And as we watch, many provinces
Are under the Emperor's wing . . . And the opulent palaces
And imperial city look so prosperous. The start
Of the splendid path appears exactly at the end
Of the Imperial Forest, the high roof of the palace, the flags
Flying, rippling…I hope to be reborn among the crags
In the verdant old green mountains, to where the eye will tend:
And put my value into being a soft white lonely cloud.
A hurricane with rain in the west part of the city,
Still lets the sun shine down upon the whole community,
The village in the sunset plain. We often each allowed
The other to drink, face to face. I often heard the accents
Of Qinyan from the Wei Jin Dynasty. Orioles twittered deep
Inside the woods, hibiscus flowers bloomed and sent their scents
Into the inner garden. I still admire the hermits who creep
Under the pines to sit in meditation, as apes give vent
To mournful cries. The monks lie on rocks, the peace to keep.

Qing Yan: it indicates a current of philosophy in the Wei Jin Dynasty which emphasized the metaphysics of Lao Tzu (Laozi) and Zhuang Tse (Zhuangzi).

121. The Night Shift with Officer Cui Hao, One Autumn Night

In the high gate of Jianli stands the night's autumn –
The palace of Chengming is waiting for dawn.
The inside door of the great royal city,
The City of Nine Gates, fills in with cold night.
In market places in towns, so many,
The regular sound of clocks breaks the quiet.
The moon looks different, across the Big Dipper,
The clouds disappear from the Milky Way.
And now the night watchman, the old timekeeper,
Ashamed to make noise, his clock-drum must play.
I'm more ashamed I'm getting duller.
We are on duty in the south path,
Our very own little sound here bringing –
Upon our horses' traces' quiet cloth,
Tiny jade pendants are dinging, dinging.

Jianli Gate: A place for officers of the secretarial court. At that time, Wang Wei held such a position.

Chengming: Chengming Palace, a place where the courtiers take rest.

Nine Gates: refers to the entire ancient Chinese palace where the Emperor lived, which had nine gates.

Tiny jade pendants dinging: In ancient China, top generals or government ministers would ride horses with jade pendant trappings. Later, people would adopt this as a symbol of magnificence.

122. I Visit the Emperor's Son-in-Law, at Cui's Pool on the Mountain

In a luxurious pavilion do the richly-ornamented female
Entertainers play seductively upon their flutes;
They belong to a select few women (hu ji), beyond the pale…
Golden bowls the barmaids use to offer the guests.
You think Female Virgin when you see the Beautiful Rock there
(This means one who cannot have a child – free and without care).
You should learn from the first Emperor to grant a title of nobility,
When you see that a pine tree will just grow up on the mountain –
These little glimpses of The Nobility they rather need –
They take off their minks in exchange for quality wine.
A man who comes here regularly shot a wild goose
And handed it in to the kitchen room before suppertime.
I hear people want to understand Taoism – what's its use?
The best way to understand it is to consider the historic time
Of Gaoyang Pool, where Shan Jian got drunk completely.
But unlike the old man who lived in Foolish Valley,
(Who gave away his calf), I just want to retreat here in austerity.

golden bowls: they are used for the barmaids to treat the guests to wine.

Beautiful Rock: located in Lian country in Guang Dong Province. The shape of this rock was very similar to the female body. Its height was about 7 feet.

glimpses of The Nobility: This story concerns a pine tree in Mt. Tai which saved the first Emperor Qin when he climbed Mt. Tai. He gave this pine a high official position in The Nobility.

Gaoyang Pool: it is said that an officer, Xi Yu, in the South Dynasty times, built a fish pool around a high dyke with bamboo, lotuses…a very beautiful place. Every time Mr. Shan Jian came here, he got drunk. Later, people called any unconventional and uninhibited meeting place (or banquet or party) "Gaoyang Pool."

Foolish Valley: see footnote for poem 98.

123. Officer Wei Lives on the Mountain

When you tour the mountain and river,
You find right here a splendid place,
A place that no one has seen, ever:
The big gully stream turns around to race
Along like flying footsteps on the stairs,
But if you want to enter my gate, you will climb
The mountain. In the kitchen the cook prepares
A meal all of bamboo ingredients: sublime.
Your official seal and its silk ribbon
Have been put beside the scenery
(Painted upon the low-hanging rattan)
When you've resigned from your high degree,
Reputation, who'll know when my suffering began?

124. Three Elegies to Prefecture Chief Du Xiwang

(1)
The Emperor's order to go out to battle in the West
You accepted as Prefecture Chief, to guard the peace
In the North, like Old General Li Guang, the best
In Yunzhong. You captured in hand the enemy's
General riding his white horse, and you occupied
The (ethnic minority) Tubo's castles. I suddenly see –
Sadly – burial objects like the straw dogs beside
And surrounding you, and I hear about your glory
As a Prefecture Chief…you passed away, the world merely
Retains your biography in its library, like "Zuozhuan."
But like Bu Shang's, who can inherit your reputation?

(2)
Now you are buried with golden gifts from the Emperor
And your wife has accompanied you to your stone manor.
She was very sad, dressed in robes in a pheasant pattern,
Holding onto the decorated coffin, waiting for dawn.
The town people were mournful, the funeral bands
And horse's neighing echoed down the river lands,
As if I heard you're a traveler at Longshang, on a quest;
You face your wife, crying to go out to battle in the West.

(3)
Now the hearse with burial objects departs the city gate,
And the coffin travels toward the cemetery and the grave.
You as Prefecture Chief leave behind a golden seal
But since then your wife will give up the officer deal –
The silk pattern cart and the trooping flag, to decay they went,
And the military music, left in the cold graveyard, will be silent.
The West, where you passed away, the tomb's tree grows toward,
And you'll always have the gratitude of the imperial court.

(1) Yunzhong: please see footnote of poem 26.

(1) Tubo or Tufan (618-842): an ancient Tibetan nation established as a State, especially in the Tang Dynasty. Tubo was very strong and always infringed on the frontier. There were many battles. Finally the Emperor brought his daughter The Princess to marry the King of Tubo in order to keep peace on the frontier.

(1) Zuozhuan: the famous history edited or written by Zuo Qiuming, a blind man who lived in the Spring and Autumn period. All the stories are anecdotes from the Spring and Autumn period. This is the world's first chronological book.

(1) straw dogs: ancient people used straw to make dog icons as sacrificial offerings.

(1) Bu Shang: also call Zi Xia, a disciple of Confucius. He was born in Jin State, but he moved to Wei State and set up a private school teaching Confucianism.

(2) stone manor: Shi Jiao, a manor in Qi State in the Spring and Autumn period. A "stone manor wife" means an honourable wife.

(2) a pheasant pattern: indicating, in ancient China, a noble lady's dress.

(2) *Longshang:* a region presently referring to the northern area of Shaanxi Province and the western part of Gansu Province in the Tang Dynasty era.

125. Visiting Li Ji's House

The gate is closed; it seems he's at leisure.
By the gate, the grass looks rather yellow.
No cart passes by, there's no horse manure;
I go down the lane to visit the old fellow.
I hear some barking and from the cold woods
The dogs rush forth; then I see you come out
To meet me, and you, not looking too good,
Without hair clasps, disheveled throughout,
Hand me a "Taoist book" for a start
(Absolutely, we both have the same heart)
We put up with poverty, enjoy episteme;
Resign the official positions, freely dream,
Like Xie Tiao resigning his governorship
At Yi Cheng; but we're both aware of it,
And we both return to the Luoyang Group –
A hermit's place – for a bowl of hot soup.

Xie Tiao (464-499): a very famous writer and poet of the South Dynasty era. He and another poet, Xie Lingyun, created Shan Shui (mountain and water) poetry and the Yong Ming style of literature.

Luoyang Group: another name for the White Community. Please see the footnote of poem 99.

126. For Pei Di

We haven't met; at least, I know that I'm
Sure we haven't met for a long, long time.
Every day I walk to the end of the stream
And I always remember, as in a kind of dream,
Us walking beside each other past a wall,
Hand in hand together; that's the symbol –
We're very close – heart to heart;
I sigh, as we're currently apart.
I remember you still, back at the start…
What, you know, do you think of yearning?
It's so deep, like some question turning.

127. A Song to the Pine Trees at the Xinqin Prefecture

You grew up on the mountain and coated it green,
You stretched so many miles – it is endless, even.
Now I meet you again – you know although
I didn't see you, you were always in my heart.
You should understand, my heart feels aglow,
Always focused on yours, though we're apart,
As you are noble and unsullied, alone or in crowds,
You stand straightly, upright from the start;
That's something different from the drifting clouds.

Xinqin Prefecture: presently in Shenmu County in Shaanxi Province.

128. Visiting Great Master Xuan

It's not worth mentioning my time of youth, and it may
Have been too late when I understood the Buddha's way.
How could the way be possible if the years have gone?
It's fortunate that I can cultivate my moral character –
And I swear never to be a meat lover, chewing on and on,
No longer winding the Net of the World ever tighter,
No longer reposing on the official's undeserved reputation,
But keeping the Sunyata practices without any restriction.
I've heard of the great master of your name for a long time;
Now I'm here, incense burning and reverence to combine.
I see you keep to your room, in a state both awake and asleep;
Not caring if all the world affairs go wrong, you just go deep.
I hear the early oriole's song twittering in the high wicker
And the spring raindrops' tick-tacks in the long corridor;
Under the bed, clogs like the hermit Run Ji's I can see.
By the window, a cane stands, a "Qiong bamboo cane"…
Like Dharma's power, your great behaviour none can explain,
And I understand the world of difference between you and me.
You concentrate on the dharma essence, its sway and pull.
You would like to take conducive Buddhism on a way to be –
Neither dying nor being born, to exhort all the people.

Master Xuan: a great disciple of zen master Pu Ji in the Tang Dynasty. He lived in the Wa Guan temple in what is presently Nanjing City in Jiangsu Province.

Sunyata: a Buddhist word in the Barry language. It means Emptiness – no creation, only calmness and extinction.

Run Ji: refers to wooden clogs. The story is from *The Book of Jin.* Ruan Fu liked making clogs and Zu Shi liked to collect jewelry. One day when a guest visited Zu Shi's house and was collecting his jewelry, he noticed Zu Shi rushing to hide two cases of jewelry behind him. When the guest visited Ruan Fu's House, he saw Ruan was simply making clogs and never cared about visitors, but kept a very calm face and whispered, "How many clogs can I make in the rest of my life?" Later, people used this story to express the nature of hermit life.

Qiong bamboo cane: a cane that used a good quality bamboo in its manufacture. This cane came from Qiong, a place called Yibin city, in Sichuan Province.

129. The Four Sages in Jizhou

(1) Officer Cui

You resign and return to the farmland.
Oh. How like a great sage you are!
When you were young but could understand,
You had been to a chivalrous person afar,
And you became a Confucian scholar.
When you were getting old, you planned
To retreat to East Mountain, spend a hermit life,
And did, in that corner of the world, follow through.
I heard you play with birds, those lives so brief…
I wish I could drive a raft, spend a hermit life with you.

(2) Officer Cheng

You wear a sword with rare ornaments
And model rich, fashionable garments,
And live in a very luxurious domicile
With a white-jade-decorated dining hall,
As an assistant to the king, no less,
Like old Prince Ping Yuan's guest.
You do often go to the house of the King
But in your home, the song girl still sings,
Like in old Handan's charming refuge.
You even sit on an equal footing to
The proud lords and willful dukes who
Communicate with a spot of chivalric sense.
However, at middle age, and hence,
You are getting somewhat less appreciation,
So you make a seeming illness your defence
And only hold this tiny official position.

(3) To the two hermits, Zheng and Huo

In the capital, those young sparks mostly were born
With silver spoons in their mouths, we know,
Like the old families of Mr. Jin and Zhang, who adorn

The Han Dynasty. It's very lucky, even so.
They have the ancestral inheritance – there's a favour
Therefore, they can be granted from the Emperor.
Even though they're in childhood, and haven't had real study,
They live a rich life in a splendid house and live marvellously,
Never worrying that nobody recommended them to the Emperor –
The way it is for those who spend a hermit's life, like any scholar.
For example, Mr. Zheng, living with stream and rock till he gets old,
Or Mr. Huo, on a far hill at peace, never disgracing himself, never bold.
They fill the hill with herbalism and sell the herbs at market,
Never doing bargaining, always accepting whatever they get.
And then they write books of achievement – ten thousand words.
When they take rest in a tree shadow, they always lean towards
The healthy tree, and when at the river to drink, they always
Choose the clear water. As for me, I am a slag; let's just say
It's not worth mentioning. But, though such is my bent,
For these two sages, who can give them a bad comment?

(1) *Officer Cui:* a military officer who kept records and followed the King or a General.

(1) *drive a raft:* an expression meaning to retire from the world.

(2) *Officer Cheng*: an officer called Wen Xue, in charge of editing articles or historical work in the palace. His surname is Cheng.

(2) *white jade decorated hall*: rich man's house.

(2) *Prince Ping Yuan's guest*: please see the footnote of poem 45.

(2) *old Handan's charming refuge:* street walking women in Handan.

(3) *Masters Zheng and Huo:* hermits in Ji Zhou (Jining in Shandong Province)

(3) *Mr. Jin and Zhang:* high class officers in the Han Dynasty. Jin indicates Jin Ridan: an attendant of the Emperor. Zhang means Zhang Shian, a General in Chief.

130. A Poem for the Prince of Qi's Contest: *"To a Night Banquet at Wei Xiang Pool on the Mountain"*

At Mount Wei, in Jia's night banquet,
The high and noble mink fur hats file in;
The palace girl's satin curtains open…
In the valley, the flowers' colours are met
By the radiant glowing of the soft pink light.
The moon and the mountain shine up the night,
Like a cavernous room with a small light shining within.
The thick greens hide the screen windows; it looks dim;
The falls pass through into the living space. It feels cool.
Furthermore, at the night banquet, we appreciate the duel
Between the dancing and the singing performances…
Please do not deeply worry on your way home, yes?

Wei Xiang: a poet and officer in Tang Dynasty. He built a pool on the mountain and named it "Wei Xiang Pool on the Mountain."

mink fur hats: signifying high officials and noble lords.

palace girl: a maid in the imperial palace.

131. Climbing to the Bianjue Temple

The bamboo path runs from the early steps to Bodhisattva
But the lotus summit comes from the Theravada state.
From the temple's window: the whole San Chu. I saw a
River beyond the forest, the Jiujiang, smooth as slate.
I sit cross-legged on the soft grass cushion,
And hear pines whispering a buddha's voice.
I came here like a man leaving for seclusion
But outside the Bodhisattva Ten-Stage choice,
So I know I can only watch, be sworn
To watch, the world to understand: "unborn."

the early steps to Bodhisattva: there are ten stages to reach Buddhahood:

1. Stage One is called The Joyous (path of seeing).
2. Stage Two is called The Stainless (deeds of ethics).
3. Stage Three: The Luminous, the light maker. (There's nothing to be gained through anger and resentment.)
4. Stage Four: The Radiant. (This stage eliminates laziness and increases the ability to practice meditation for extended periods of time.)
5. Stage Five: Very Hard To Conquer (difficult to overcome): this means one has completed the training of this level and has profound wisdom and insight that are difficult to surpass or undermine, according to Nagarjuna.
6. Stage Six: The Training Toward: understanding "signless-ness."
7. Stage Seven: The Far Going: the number of his qualities have increased, and moment by moment he can enter the equipoise of cessation.
8. Stage Eight: The Unshakeable (immovable). Bodhisattvas overcome all afflictions regarding signs and their minds are always completely absorbed in the Dharma.
9. Stage Nine: The Good Mind: Bodhisattvas move quickly toward awakening.
10. Stage Ten: The Cloud of Dharma: Like a cloud that pours the rain of truth upon the earth.

Throughout this poem, Wang Wei suggests some of the ten stages to us: *the bamboo path* is like the First stage; *the lotus summit* is the Second stage: he sees the mountain as a lotus; *the temple's window* is like the Third stage; he stands to watch the scenery in the world; *the Jiu Jiang, smooth as slate* – the Fourth stage? Then he starts to take his attention back to the present meditation. So he suddenly understands that it's very hard to reach the tenth stage without watching the world because the Dharma of Buddha exists *in* the world!

Theravada state: refers to a state of Nirvana in the teachings of Buddha. This instance indicates a temple.

San Chu: refers to three regions in the south, east and west of Chu State in the Spring and Autumn and Warring States periods. Presently it refers to the two provinces of Hunan and Hubei, and parts of Jiangsu, Anhui, Henan – three other provinces.

Jiujiang: in ancient times called Xun Yang Chai Sang or Jiang Zhou, presently Jiujiang City in Jiangxi Province. In the north, it is close to Poyang Lake, the biggest fresh lake in China, very famous in southern China as the major tea and rice market.

"unborn": please see poem 118's footnote.

132. The Owner of Qianta temple

Lodge in seclusion and – meet a festival!
A ship in a long journey has to stop,
Its window by the Bian River Temple.
Cocks and dogs, scattering in the ruins, hop
By the temple's door. The boat makes much ado;
It has been traveling long, all the way from Chu.
The local remote fields are covered by
The shadows of the elm and mulberry
(Long shadows from the setting sun).
I live right here; I don't see anyone,
Just the pillow and mat, living an emptiness
(In clouds and mist, where more is less.)

Qianta temple: an old temple close to the Bian River in Henan in the Tang Dynasty

Bian River: a river running through Xingyang City in Henan Province. It belongs to the eastern end of the Tong Ji River. The head of this river from northern Ying Yang connects to the Yellow River, then runs through to parts of Henan and Anhui provinces, and finally merges into the Huai River.

Chu (1115-223 BC): a feudal state of the Western Zhou Dynasty, one of The Seven States in the Warring States Period. Its strongest stage was in the Spring and Autumn period, when King Zhuang became a strong leader and established a great State. He also became one of The Five Hegemons and wiped up Yue State and expanded its borderline to the Jiang Nan (the south shore of the Yangtze River). Finally, it was defeated by the State of Qin. Bian River belonged to Chu in the Spring and Autumn and Warring States periods.

133. Visiting Zen Master Cheng Ru's Temple at Mount Song

Wu Zhuo and Tian Qin are brothers in *The Bodhisattva*, a Buddhist story
But here in your temple at The Mountain it's like a summit, so clearly…
When you eat a meal and knock the Qing, the crows will come down
From their nests to help you eat your meal together – they're always around.
When you go out, your steps come with the sounds of fallen leaves.
The water's from the buddha that moistens your incense burner table;
Buddha's flowers fall from heaven, to make for your stone bed, sheaves.
And how can a tall pine grow in a deep cave? It's like the Indian Lao Tzu fable.

Master Cheng Ru: a great master in the Tang Dynasty. He became a monk at 21 years of age. And he received great respect from the Emperor, who gave him the name "great moral master." He reformed Buddhism and set up the Coffin Tower system for the burial and honouring of monks.

Wu Zhuo: (Asengaha), an Indian Buddhist who created the Yogacara school of Mahayana Buddhism. He was an older brother of Tian Qin.

*Tian Qin: (*Pasapando) a younger brother of Wu Zhuo. They were all Bodhisattvas in ancient India.

Qing: a percussive musical instrument in Buddhist temples, of a shape very similar to an alms bowl.

The water from the buddha: this artifact depicts a story from the "Hui Yuan biography:" once upon a time, Master Hui Yuan moved to Mount Lu and lived in the Ling Quan Temple. The river was far from there, and it was very inconvenient if you wanted a drink of water. He used his cane to poke the ground, praying: if this place can allow me living and teaching Buddha here, please let this wasted land produce a spring. Unexpectedly, his speech over, water began running out of the ground.

Buddha's flower: it was said when Shakyamuni became a Buddha and taught the Buddha's way, mandala flowers dropped from heaven like rain.

Indian Lao Tzu fable: the legend is that Lao Tzu reincarnated in India and became Buddha. They called him The Old Man.

134. In Honour of Officer Su, Who Came to My Villa At Lantian, but Left Quickly

My poor house is close to the head of the valley,
But the tree layers around the desolate village,
And that stone path of mine – it's a very great pity –
Brought you to suffer a wasted pilgrimage.
I know a house on the mountain where
You could live if you're willing to stay there.
In winter, fishing boats get stuck, the ferry freezes,
And only hunting fires burn across the boundless land.
From out of mere clouds, a clock sound breezes,
As if I hear the apes crying, and I understand.

Officer Su: he was an officer who served in the Yu department (the Gong branch, in charge of city gardens). His position was to be in charge of the officials overlooking vegetables, wood, fires, or hunting. He visited Wang Wei's house at Wang River and left his poetry; then Wang Wei responded with this poem to apologize for his absence.

135. For Officers Yan and Xu Who Visited Me Though I Was Absent

As an official, of course, I seldom enjoy a holiday.
As I live poorly, it's rare, of course, that friends visit.
When you come, occasionally, to visit, say,
Just as I've gone out in the Lan Yu, it's not antisocial, is it?
It's not about avoiding your white robes…
Please forgive my family – they didn't know glutinous millet
Should have been cooked as a treat for your honourable personalities.
What of the person who only knows sweeping the poor wooden door?
Actually, if you are willing to drink only the teas,
You may as well ride your horses here; return at once, for sure.

A humorous and fairly ironical poem!

officers Yan and Xu: both were officers close to the imperial family.

Lan Yu: a palanquin usually carried by 4 people. It is used here as an idiom meaning: to go to the office.

white robes: (or white clothes) refers to a minor officer or an adjutant to a senior officer.

the glutinous millet: a great treat for honoured guests.

sweeping the poor wooden door: someone inexperienced who only knows his family affairs.

136. Murong Cheng Visits, Carrying a Vegetarian Meal

The official hat is put upon the small black sheepskin table –
I linger around my home idly, even tired of writing poetry.
By the door I watch, but I only know the hermit. I'm able,
According to my calculation, to say my age is seventy three
And that I've understood the six Dharmakayas in my life time.
It's made of a special wood, "Ling -Shou Mu," this cane of mine,
And it was given by the King, who surely has his scruples.
And there's the zizania rice meal, cooked by my disciples.
Ungraciously, you bring to me a vegetarian meal and wine…
But we accept it, happy and enjoying eating – we won't decline.

Murong Cheng: Wang Wei's friend, also a lay Buddhist.

six Dharmakayas: The Mahayana Buddha realized that the Buddha's body has 3 two-sided parts: Dharmakaya, Sambhogakaya, and Nirmanakaya.

"Ling-Shou Mu:" a kind of bush that grows on Mt. Guo (Shuozhou City in Shanxi Province). Its wood has a natural quality that is ideal for the making of canes. In ancient times, as a symbol for long life, the Emperor always sent these canes to his old officials.

137. Thanks for the Visit, Governor Zheng

The sunshine in the late spring days
Yields a sky purely clear and bright –
The fields of grasses and the woods look fresh.
In front of the well, the mirror's haze,
I polish away, almost but not quite,
Like the immortal Fu Ju, but it does impress.
Under the trees, I'm a hermit in the farm garden.
The bustling horse-drawn cart that's come to visit
Makes the poor lane shake, quietly but powerfully.
2 boy servants accompany me – an old man among men.
My chef only cooks food if coarse rice meal is in it.
Excuse my home – poor it is, like Ruan Xian / Ruan Ji's.

Governor Zheng: A governor of Guo Zhou Prefecture, presently Nan Chong County in Sichuan Province.

Fu Ju: said to be an immortal, he lived in Yan State. He often polished the mirrors of others, but actually would take opportunities to give people herbs to cure their illnesses.

A hermit in the farm garden: it refers to Chen Zhong Zi, mentioned in poem 99.

Ruan Xian and Ruan Ji: theirs was a very poor home. In Ruan Xian and his uncle Ruan Ji's time, every year on July the 7th, the custom was to hang your clothes outside. There were two kinds of people living on his street – the rich people on the north end and the poor on the south. On July 7, the rich people would hang out their silks or other fineries, but the Ruans, south enders, could only hang out their coarse cloth underwear, of a shape very similar to a calf's nose. They're in fact called, "calf nose pants."

138. Overlooking the Suburbs of Liangzhou

In these suburbs very few farms have been dared;
It's rare to see a neighbour at a boundary line.
The activity of praying to the demon is shared
Among those dancing trippingly on wine...
People are blowing on the Xiao flute;
The drum's racing, the sacrifice to the demon's
On. They're splashing the wine of newt
Upon the straw dogs, and the incense burns;
Worship of the wooden immortals is due.
Wild witches are dancing frequently...
Of course, their silk stockings bring the hues
Of all colours to the world, naturally.

Xiao flute: a vertical bamboo flute, a musical instrument of ancient China

straw dogs: please see the footnote of poem 124.

139. Boating the Bayshore

Obviously, “the sky of autumn” in Autumn is so bright;
Besides, I am far from the crowd world of no insight.
Boating the bayshore, with a crane, having a good swim,
I’m between the water and sand and sky and sea bottom.
And furthermore, with the mountain out of the cloud,
In the evening, the stream water is so clear and loud.
And facing later the bright moon, I feel so leisurely.
Tonight, I would like to let the boat drift, take it easy,
Moving without will with the dreamy stream forever,
Not thinking of returning to a home I can’t remember.

140. Listening to the Song of the Oriole at the Palace

In spring, the trees surround the palace walls;
As the dawn commences, the oriole sings in the lane.
It's so surprising when its song suddenly stalls–
Because I approach. But when I move, it sings again.
It hides in the leaves and bathes in the shimmering dew.
It climbs out of the flowers, flies from the Palace, out of view.
Weiyang Palace – tourists return, but don't understand.
I hear the twittering, and start to miss my homeland.

Weiyang Palace: created in the time of the first Emperor, Liu Bang of the Han Dynasty, who lived there until the time of the Tang Dynasty. It has always been a palace of the Emperor. It has a 1,140 year history. Its old address was in the Wei Yang district in Xi'an City in Shaanxi Province.

141. For Murong Cheng

Stop-and-go, I return from the west,
And stop my cart at your gate to ask for you.
Like Che Yin, you're a man who's the best
At sociability, at *hello and how do you do.*
Your two official horsemen drive my cart,
And a tall doorman opens for me the door,
And they tell me even you have a start
At getting old now. You'll go to the frontier
(Saibei) although you're unwilling to leave
This secluded place of yours, and must grieve.
I ask the liveried doorman here to tell you –
A person with noble intentions, like Hu Qiu Zi:
I (pretending my surname's Meng) come to meet you.

Che Yin: was born and raised in the East Jin Dynasty, and became a keen student who liked to read and study. But his family was very poor, often lacking oil to keep a lamp burning. He made a unique light to help with his night reading, using a white cloth bag full of many fireflies. When he became an officer, he developed a high reputation and never neglected the social community or to attend parties. Finally, he was framed by Si Ma Yuan Xian and driven to suicide.

Saibei: an old place name in ancient China, referring to northern sections of the Great Wall. As well it means a frontier between the Han Nation and minor outlying nations.

Hu Qiu Zi: born in the State of Zheng in the Spring and Autumn period, he learned through belonging to Huang (The Yellow Emperor), Lao (Lao Tzu), and Tao (Purposive Taoism and Instrumental Taoism). He had the highest morality, it is agreed.

pretending my surname's Meng: refers to Zhuangzi, a Taoist in the Spring and Autumn period. He was born in Meng Place (presently in Mengcheng County in Henan Province) in the state of Song. Later people also called him Sir Meng. Song State was a great country in the Spring and Autumn Period. The Three Sages were born there: Mo Tse (Mozi) who created Moism; Zhuang Tse (Zhuangzi) a great representative of Taoism; and Huizi (who created The Logicians). Song State is also the ancestral home of Confucius.

142. A Visit to the Tomb of the First Emperor, Qin

The old tomb's found now atop a green hill,
And the tomb itself looks as if its palace
Was where the seven luminaries lived until
Separated, and the Milky Way's old face
Even appears on the grave in the grave yard.
The Chen star fills it in; it likes the river and sea.
It's impossible that humans can be barred
Or trespass. And there no spring can be,
And so the gold goose never can return.
Furthermore, I heard the pine woods sound
Like worried knots, that somehow learn.
I don't doubt that the pine that's still around,
Given to first Emperor Qin, when his status was much less,
(A senior officer's at that time) now too knows sadness.

seven luminaries: in ancient China, this collective name included the Sun, Moon, Venus (Taibai), Jupiter (Taisui), Mercury (the Chen star), Mars (Yinghuo), and Saturn (the Tian star).

gold goose: a sacrificial object made of gold in the shape of a goose, a valuable symbol.

143. A Poem for an Unrecognized Scenario

Submits a report to the Bei Que (imperial court)
But doesn't get any response the next morning.
Plants seed in the land
But gets nothing when the harvest comes.
Emperor holds a large meeting (over a hundred people attending)
But doesn't include this person.
You would like to have a gate like five bigwig Marquis,
But in the heart, there is dislike.
Only can put in at Heshuo (the north shore of the Yellow Sea)
And drink wine from a friend (& depend on this friend for a living)
… It's living like Mao Ling; does anyone think it is safely?
For the moment, let's climb the mountain and cross the river,
Not caring if the spring wind blows the poplar or wicker.
Nowadays, people's behaviour is more selfish,
So who is there to understand this unhappiness in the heart?
There's a hope to benefit mankind someday, and then leave off…
Is a man not a man? How could it be in name only!

Mt. Nan: also called Mt. Zhongnan. Please see footnote of poem 61.

living like Mao Ling: please see the footnote of poem 119.

Not caring if the spring wind blows the poplar or wicker: concern about family worries.

144. When I Send Off Cui Hao to Mount Nan

We say goodbye on a desultory corner of this city we are in.
I do not even know where or when we might ever meet again…
You know here the Fall osmanthus will cover the mountain –
Please do not let me wait for you until the flowers fall like rain.

145. A Poem Without a Title

We look at each other and hate to say goodbye.
It’s a cheerless nightfall, the spreading tide is high.
Finally, we say adieu, and lingeringly,
We shake hands tightly, affectionately –
Then from the islet the moon jumps to the sky.

146. For He Si, Who Gave Me the Present of a Hood

You present me a hood made of ko-hemp cloth, that was
Like a hermit's hood that spread a wonderful goodness.
This present is more treasured than the best gold.
This hood, this hermit one, could let me enfold
A feeling to embrace a reclusion unending.
After I meet the Emperor in the morning,
I will hang this up at home for a while
In the evening after a bath and then I'll
Clip it on again. Sitting here with it I feel
The petty world has gone so very far away
And so I think about escaping, to quietly steal
Away to a hermit life with you, and there to stay.

147. Sending Off Qiu Wei to Tangzhou

You will go to Wan and Luo, and then Tangzhou, the famous city,
And many world affairs, like a tangled skein, will be harassing you,
And I can imagine how hard it is for you (sympathy, this, not pity)
To be travelling. Your worries come from all the old and new
Directions that link to the Han River, that area of bothers.
Your speeches, inevitably, will follow the many others.
Look at the pagoda tree's colour: so gloomy, even in daytime,
And the poplar blossoms, provoking the late Spring, benign –
In the morning I would like to send you off, as you now wear
The Emperor's special, official-pattern robes to go there.

Wan and Luo: a short form of Wan Nanyang and Luoyang, locations in Henan Province.

Tangzhou: presently Miyang County in Henan Province.

148. Sending Off a Friend Returning to the South

Now in the south, the spring's already gone
And seeing the wild geese has gotten rare.
Flying past the three rivers (Li, Xiang, Yuan),
They have all vanished into northern air.
The Han River is so vast it even connects heaven.
You my friend, as a single guest, will now return
To your homeland, Ying City. There, in Xun country,
The rice shoot's growing very well, offering its bounty,
As the Gu rice is getting quite ripe enough to harvest.
I miss you in this North, and by the door I often invest
Time into gazing towards the South, as if I see you
(Like Lao Lai Zi in motley dress, who pretended to
Be a child to make his parents happy) returning as due.

Ying City: a Capital of Chu State in the Spring and Autumn and Warring States periods.

Xun Country: a small state close to Chu in the Spring and Autumn and Warring States periods.

Lao Lai Zi: a hermit in Chu State in the Spring and Autumn and Warring States periods. He was very filial, and though 70 years old, still wore colourful clothes to pretend to be a child to make his parents happy.

149. Sending Off Sun Er

At the suburbs, who sends you off?
You are my friend – I know you're soft
On the Dharma of Taoism, flexible, like a beginner.
Me, I know scholars from Zou and Lu Country,
And the cleverest person from Luoyang City.
We lean on the cool grass enjoying a farewell dinner,
Then in the dusk your traveling cart rolls up the dirt road.
After you leave, how lonely, the mountain and the river!
I watch your last trace fondly, tears sprinkling my robe.

scholars from Zou and Lu: Mencius was born in Zou State and Confucius was born in Lu State. Later, this idiom came to mean a famous place that produces a great person.

cleverest person from Luoyang City: refers to Jia Yi, who was born there. Please see the footnote of poem 61. Later, this became an idiom for clever people who show talent when quite young.

150. I Am Pleased Zu San Lodges in My Home

In front of my door, you arrive as if a Luoyang Guest,
Dismount the horse, brush dust off your traveling dress.
Oh my friend, I hope this trip was worth it for you,
As I mostly close my door after talking's through.
You and I are just pedestrians, returning to my home –
A deep lane, isolated, where one can write a poem…
The snow-thick slopes draw silver from the setting sun.
In the early years, we both played the classmate part
But right now, it seems all parts have come undone.
Where will you go when you ride the wealthy cart?

a Luoyang Guest: please see the footnotes of poems 149 and 61 about Zhi Zi, born in Luoyang City.

151. A Qing Rhyme Poem to Send Off Governor Zhao to Daizhou

As the next Governor you will bring your military to the new scene;
In the sky I saw, I thought, the General Star moving from Heaven.
On the earth of my country, the wicker strands recharge with green;
The Diao Dou kettles sound on toward a thousand miles, then ten,
And the troops line up to issue out of Jingjing Pass.
You leave the booming capital city now en masse
To serve our country, the enemies to fight and try.
As a General you'll never become pedantic or dry,
By the window writing, reading poems until you die.

Qing Rhyme Poem: an ancient Chinese style of poetry of 8 lines with identical rhymes on the 1st (sometimes), 2nd, 4th, 6th, and 8th lines.

the General Star: ancient Chinese astronomy attributed various qualities to the stars, and if a large star appeared, it foretold successful war.

Diao Dou kettles: used both for cooking in daytime and for sounding an alarm or the hours at night.

Jingjing Pass: an important frontier in the Tang Dynasty, presently inside Jingjing County in Hebei Province.

152. A Late Spring Thought from the Boudoir

The new dress – its colour looks so pitiful, for all that.
The setting sunlight spreads up the curtains, screens.
The woman's virtuous scent refreshes the rich mat.
The jade stairs give the wall's shadow a jade sheen.
It's Spring: insects fly around the window, the door's net,
At dusk, sparrows hide in the branches and the bowers.
I face the nightfall, which, of course, means worries calling.
By the boudoir's window, I watch the peach, plum flowers
Falling.

153. Magnolia Valley

In autumn the summit of the mountain
Blocks exactly half the setting sun.
Birds chase their lovers ahead so fast,
And soon disappear into the distant forest.
The glow of sunset shines a golden light
Upon the woodland greens, their heights.
The air is clear, the forest mist is lifting;
No night fog's on the mountain, drifting.

154. To Qiu Wei, Upon Parting

My return leads back beyond white clouds,
And I must ride this horse away from you.
It's like the mountain wall gathering crowds
Of clouds that build and build in altitude.
Today and tomorrow go on as ever
But the heart has leisure? Ah, never.
Thank you for the sendoff, the official dinner,
Where you said to me repeatedly,
Please come back in spring, before it's summer,
And the dust lies heavy on the leaves.
I look back to you, step by step you see,
Going forward home, but slowly, slowly.

155. Saying Goodbye to Wang River Villa

This villa I built for my mother, who loved me from the start.
Unwilling to part am I, but I have to drive this horse cart,
And leave the deep pine forest, melancholy in my heart.
Suffering separation from the green mountain, I must aver,
Without it I'm not able to do anything about the blue water,
The blue water of time, containing all the memories, astir.

156. For Zu San (Writing this Poem in My Office at Qi Zhou)

A spider hangs his webs upon the empty windows;
Below the windows' stairs, a lonely cricket's singing.
He's like us, a gentleman…what are *we* to be doing?
Now the year has almost gone, the cold wind blows.
And there are no people in this house, huge and tall,
But I really cannot say that I live in isolation.
It's closed, the empty gate some way along the wall,
Though it's been manned for a long duration.
The setting sun shines in the grass of autumn.
Although we've exchanged mail quite recently,
It's not the same as being with one you can see.
A thousand long miles have kept us separated
By rivers, and high mountain passes antiquated.
You stayed as a hermit at Ying River, it appears,
Until last year – then returned to your hometown.
Although our friendship has lasted 20 years,
We could not get one day to meet, we found.
You have lived with poverty and illness
A long time. As always, I keep missing you.
In mid-autumn you could not finesse
A visit, but late autumn now sees you get through.
A few days before we meet, could our luck be turning?
Every day I feel for you the unforgotten yearning.

Zu San: a well-known poet friend of Wang Wei's.

Ying River (Yingchuan): the name of a prefecture that began in the Qin Dynasty. Presently Yuzhou City in Henan Province. Due to the Ying River running through it, it is named Yingchuan Prefecture.

157. A Poem to Qian Qi at Parting

Though your official position's to be lower,
You'll still retain your own distinctive personality –
All the high white clouds will inevitably return with you.
And then when you become a senior officer
You'll still obey your parents faithfully, like Lu Ji.
You'll guard the mountain; avoid Cai Wei seclusion, too.
The bird in evening will find again its nest;
The new times wait for you to open their door.
Even the clouds and the Milky Way attest:
A good friend's waiting at the Imperial Court.

Qian Qi: a famous poet, one of the big talents of the Da Li period (Nov 766 – Dec 799) of the Tang Dynasty.

Lu Ji: an officer in Wu State in the Three Kingdoms period, a character in a very famous story: when he was 6 years old he followed his father to meet King Yuan Shu, and Yuan gave him 3 tangerines, which he hid in his sleeves. Unfortunately, when he bent his knees to say goodbye to Yuan Shu, the tangerines dropped on the floor. Yuan laughed and asked him why he hid the tangerines? He courageously replied that he was going to bring them home to his mother. He became an example of family loyalty and his story was collected in *The Book of Fealty.*

Cai Wei: gatherer of firewood. Please see the footnote for poem 43 (Bo Yi and Shu Qi).

158. To Qiwu Qian

You hold the "Hu" to go to palace, through your hopes and fears,
And you have been in service to the Emperor these several years.
You make official edicts at the Imperial Library
As senior imperial officer, you often are at liberty
To join in discussions at the senior office building.
You make poetry that's appropriate and joy-bringing,
But it doesn't pump you up – arrogance you escape,
And you relate to others with all lack of the red tape.
Plenty skilled in the eastern jin, the Jian Zuo characters,
You have great concern for Jian'an style, in particular.
Most of your art is elegant in style, independent work –
You take this style to clean the current poetry murk.
Severe winter comes and all the woods decay;
The Yi and Luo Rivers run so clear, on and away.
Now, the wide Wei River runs underneath the ice;
The Tong Pass has just closed in snow. My advice:
When the lotus root comes back, and woods wear their green sash,
The dirt of an official hat will be waiting for you to come to wash.

Hu: very similar to a sceptre, a long, narrow board made of bamboo, jade, or ivory, used to take notes when an officer meets with the Emperor.

Imperial Library...senior imperial officer: before Qi resigned his official position, he edited a book at the Imperial Library.

Jiang Zuo characters: a literary style in East Jin in the Southern Dynasty. Its representatives are Xie Tiao, Xie Lingyun, and Tao Yuanming.

Jian'an Style: in Wei Country during the Three Kingdoms period in China, 7 poets or writers created a special literary style: vigorous, crafty, and heroic yet melancholic. They all expressed the same theme: that human life is suffering and very short and that most people cannot realize their goals. This style absorbs the Yue Fu poetry of the Han Dynasty and changes the Fu in the Han Dynasty to poetry. This is the root of metrical poetry, and this style influenced Tang poetry.

Its representatives include 7 individuals and 3 members of the Cao family all of whom lived in the Jian'an period. The 7 persons: Kong Rong, Chen Lin, Wang Can, Xu Gan, Ruan Yu, Ying Yang, and Liu Zhen. The 3 Caos: Cao Cao and his two sons, Cao Pei and Cao Zhi.

Yi and Luo: refers to River Yi and River Luo. River Yi is tributaries of River Luo. River Luo is a tributary of the Yellow River, crossing over Shaanxi and Henan Provinces. This region is also called the He Luo region, and it was a cradle of the Huaxia Nation.

Wei River: Please see the footnote of poem 82.

Tong Pass: Please see the footnote of poem 48.

159. Officer Yang Is Exiled to Binzhou

Tomorrow you will leave here, to go too far away,
To the distant Mount Heng and Dongting Lake.
But how could you not face the cool moon in autumn,
And listen to an ape crying, sounding like a sad human?
I can imagine you practicing remote viewing
On islets of the northern part of the Three Xiang
With your sorrow,
Tiring of saying the huge south wind blows you naught…
You should, could, not return to the northern capital, but
I tell you now,
When the grasses get green, you will pass the Xiakou,
And boating, you'll edge by Pen City, passing through.
Because Chang Sha is a place so remote,
It could not long keep such a scholar of note
Pushed down below.
You will be hired by The Emperor like Jia Yi, and you'll belong;
You won't need to pay a visit to the ancient sage, Qu Yuan Song.

Officer Yang: an officer who managed the royal property and day to day affairs.

Binzhou: presently Bin County in Hunan Province

Mount Heng: Located in Heng Shang Country in Hunan Province, one of the Five Famous Mountains in China. It is also called Nan Yue. This is where for the first time sacrifices were offered to Heaven in Yu and Shun times. It's a place for praying to Heaven and to the genealogy of the Emperor. As well, it's a sacred place for Taoism and Buddhism.

Dongting Lake: the second largest fresh water lake, located in the northern area of Hunan Province. This lake also runs through to the Yangtze.

Xiakou: an old castle located at Mount Huanghu in Wuhan City in Hubei Province.

Pen City: in Jiujiang city In Jiangxi Province.

Jia Yi: please see the footnote of poem 61.

Qu Yuan: the first poet of Hua Xia, born in Chu in the Warring States period. When he was young, the King of Huai in Chu State believed in him and gave him a high official position as an officer close to the King. He wrote much poetry and developed the Sao poetry style but was politically marginalized by the nobility, then exiled to the remote Chang Sha in Hunan Province. After Qin occupied Ying, the capital of Chu State, Qu Yuan was rumoured to have drowned in the Mi Luo River. One legend told of his suicide; another mentioned him being hunted down. It was said the Dragon Boat Festival was set up in his memory, despite the 4,000-year-old Dragon Boat Festival long predating him. His poetry influenced the entire literature of ancient China.

160. Qi Lake

I play the Xiao flute down by the ferry of Ling Ji;
At dusk I must send my husband off away from me.
While his boat is disappearing distantly
On the fading lake, he turns his head, to see if he can…
The white cloud is rolling up the side of the green mountain.

161. A Cry to Yin Yao

How long can anyone keep themselves alive…
Finally, won't we surely all become invisible…
From right now I'll miss you till I've died…
It hurts human feelings in every way possible…
Now you have no time to bury your mother
As she's still here and you're with the other.
And you left 1 daughter who's just 10 years old.
Now we make a suburban farewell in the cold.
I hear the sound of crying rustling the air;
I see the drifting clouds growing boundless,
Even the flying bird can't be singing here.
How lonely is the procession – friendless!
Even the daytime feels so chilly and spare.
I remember when you were alive –
You asked me how you could study infinity.
Now I am very sad I've survived
But didn't encourage you to study that early,
And caused you to get, spiritually, nothing.
Now this poem about you, old friend, I bring,
Though your whole life it cannot summarize.
Are you so dissatisfied, not only in this thing?
I return to my poor house with soulful cries.

Yin Yao: A friend of Wang Wei, the year of birth and death is unknown. He was also a poet, but he was very poor. When he died, his family had no money to bury him.

162. A Poem Made on the Mountain in Early Autumn

I am an ungifted person, I dare not
Trouble the brilliant imperial court,
So I think of Dong Xi's eastern stream, going back
And keeping up the fence work around my old tract.
I have now a child married, hoping for no divorce;
How could I resign, though, so early as Shang Ping?
But I murmur at letting officialdom run its course
Until I'm way past retirement (like Tao Yuanming).
In autumn, the cricket's chirping more, as if it is rushed.
At dim dusk, the long cicada song is sorrowful and lonely.
By the wicket no visitor waits, the mountain's hushed;
In all the vast forest, I'm correlative with white clouds only.

Shang Ping (also, Shangzi): his story is from a "high quality scholar biography" by Ji Kang, in the Jin Dynasty: a man, Shang Ping from Chao Ge (Qi County in Henan Province) arranged his son's marriage, then said to his son and daughter, "From now on, you pretend I have passed on." Then he parted from his whole family and travelled from home, and finally nobody knew where he'd gone. He became an example of a person unburdened by family.

Tao Yuanming: Please see the footnotes for poems 26 and 180.

163. Sending Off Cui Jiu to Shu

Since when I sent you off before,
I have felt this more and more:
The number of old friends grows less,
And less. The farm garden door
Just closed; the housekeeper herself, yes,
Still looks back in her patterned dress,
As you go out to live abroad,
On your way to places odd,
Traveling to the Han Yi Fest…
I know you'll go – an affirmative nod –
To Jiang Han, basically as just another guest…
When do you come back here as *my* tourist?

Han Yi Festival: established in the ancient Zhou Dynasty (before the Qin), which then in the Qin Dynasty became popular. This festival is only held in northern China. Every year, somewhat like Halloween, on Oct the 1st (in the lunar calendar) in northern China, the weather gets cold, so people pray to their ancestors and burn clothing for them. Han Yi means clothes which dispel coldness.

164. I Visit Hermit Li's House, Write a Poem On His Wall

All the world is like a dream, when you are conceited;
You only sing your own song, however it is greeted.
As for your age, it's older than your tallest pine tree,
And much more than forest bamboo in your vicinity.
So you plant several herbs and the quality of them
Is pretty good; you sell it according to your price,
All fair and square yet there's no chance of a bargain,
Like ancient drug dealer Han Kang's, not so nice.
Your door only permits hermit visits like Shangzi's,
Where you toss and turn upon the mat, just ill at ease.
Even the white cloud, can it do to you as it may please?

Han Kang: Han Kang always picked up herbs and brought them to sell in the market. He never lowered his prices for anyone in need for all 30 years. Finally he secluded on Mount Ba Ling near Xi'an City in Shaanxi Province.

Shangzi (also Shang Ping): please see footnote for poem 162.

165. To Send Off Officer Lu

There is a wise man like you in our office, I stammer.
Unexpectedly, you have the ancient people's manner.
The Emperor considers the safety of the Hebei Territory,
Then makes an imperial edict asking you to join the fray…
Warfare, in conquest for the eastern lands and boundary.
You say goodbye, with both hands together, risen in front,
To the commander of this ministry, and go out to hunt.
You leave our office in Nan Gong, go down the hall…
Look, the nine tributaries of the Yellow River are all
Running out across the plains, as ever they have done,
And the seven vassal states all now belong to Qi Men.
There, only the chilly wind blows the withered mulberries,
Many more fleabanes grow up around the ancient fortress.
In a ten-thousand-mile radius, you cannot find any enemies;
The barbarian's region has been emptied, while we redress
Their recent outrages and crimes. It looks so desolate,
It's unnecessary to expend national power to defend it,
But the military still wants to send an army into war
As they seek taking wonderful credit and rich reward.
I'm unwilling to part, but I come here to send you afar;
I shake your hand tightly, and sigh about how our fate
Is so different between us! The time of your trip of state
To there and your return here (with the title of Marquis)
Would be very long – would you then still like to visit me?
A senile man like an ancient Mount Shang hermit I will be.

Nan Gong: the chancery in the Tang Dynasty. This official mechanism was established from the time of the Han Dynasty to the Song Dynasty in China: supreme government-decreed organization of administration.

Mountain Shang hermit: refers to a time when in late Qin the country was in flames, and 4 Taoists (Tang Bing, Cui Guang, Wu Shi, and Zhou Shu) moved to Mt. Shang (Shang Luo City in Shanxi Province) and Qin disappeared. They didn't want to serve the new Han Dynasty, but eventually, to become the prince's tutors, they came out of their Mt. Shang retreat. By then, they were all in their 90s and their hair and beards had all become white. Later, people called these 4 the "Mount Shang Senior Hermits."

nine tributaries: a region located in the southwest Shandong plains.

Seven States: refers to Youzhou, an area in the Tang Dynasty belonging to Qimen (presently southwest of Beijing).

166. Grateful to the Emperor

(I had already committed a crime but recovered an official position soon afterward, so I felt deeply grateful to the Emperor and expressed my feeling in this poem. And here I speak for all the absolved officers, including the prefectural governor.)

An imperial edict arrives, returns to me my official hat –
I realize the Emperor has untied me from a tragic trap.
I think now of the sun – The Emperor's brilliance is only a bit less.
The Emperor's life owes a fair-sized debt to the sky for its success.
The flowers face the happiness, they all know with a smile;
The birds meet the joyful things, they all express with a song,
Not to mention me, a human. I got a new official seal meanwhile –
The Prefectural Governor's – even though I have done wrong.
Again, I will ride a splendid horse in costly dress
Adorned with jade pendants, and go to the palace!

167. Northern Hill at Wang River
(From Wang River Collection)

At the north of great Lake Qi is the land called Bei Cha.
Miscellaneous trees were shading vermeil vines, we saw.
The river flowing slowly south is intricately wriggly,
Its flickering reflections run on through the forests dimly.

168. Poem at Yunxi Villa (Huangpu Yue's house): A Dockyard of Lotus

The lotus-gathering boat goes to pick up lotuses daily,
The sandbank is so long it causes them to come home late.
Returning at dusk, they employ the bargepole very carefully,
Even avoiding splashing water or waves that may mate,
For fear of wetting the red lotus's petals (its dress, you see).

169. I Meet Pei Di by the Rainy Wang River and Recall Mount Zhongnan

The river prevails exceedingly with its vast, cold waves.
The autumn rain is boundless, these grey weeks and days.
The sky looks dark and gloomy, the daylight disallowed.
You ask me about Mount Zhongnan's habitual ways –
In my heart I know it is located just within the white cloud.

170. A Poem for Wei Mu

You and I are people with black-eye appreciation
(Eyes like Ruan Jie's eyes). Not true for everyone.
And we both have the free heart of a hermit
(Like a white cloud heart). Should time permit…
If you do not go to Dong Shan (a hermitage),
Time will cause our mountain's spring grass
To grow deeply, from the valley to the pass.

Wei Mu: about this person's life little is known.

black-eye appreciation: the idiom comes from Ruan Jie, a distinguished man in the East Jin Dynasty. It is said Mr. Ruan Jie could show his eyes two ways. When he met a vulgar person he would roll his eyes back to show only the whites, showing that he disliked talking with him. If he liked a person, he would show him his normal black eyes.

171. A Poem for Pei Di Again When I'm Caged in Puti Temple

If I could escape this little cage, I would go off in a huff
And say goodbye to the noisy world and its stupid bluff.
I will walk with a cane made from a chenopodium stem –
Leisurely, I'll return to the Peach Garden, forgetting them.

Written after being captured and forced to serve in the government of the rebels, who'd given him an officer he couldn't refuse (because if you are unfamiliar with the Godfather, he'd be dead and then unable to refuse).

172. A Poem for General Pei Min

Your waist wears the treasured sword of the seven stars,
And your shoulder the sculpted bow, on it, printed wars:
A hundred battles' exploits. When I meet you, I am proud
To hear you have captured the sly enemies in the cloud.
I just understand this principle –
Heaven still has itself a General.

Pei Min: a man who lived in the Kaiyuan time in the Tang Dynasty. He fought several battles against such enemies as Tupo, Qidan, Xiqiang, and he was made a Great General by the Emperor. His highest skill was in sword dancing. He was also called "Saint Sword."

173. I Send Off Officer Wei

I want to follow you, a general again,
To capture the barbarian's commander –
We know him as the King of Youxian –
And ride the horse to battle over there,
To the battlefield, Juyan, where old courage began.
However right now I'm only able to imagine you
As an imperial envoy, like the Han Dynasty had, too.
Standing alone at Xiaoguan, you'll watch, tomorrow,
The setting sun fall on the lonely castle, with a sorrow.

officer Wei: an officer in charge of jail affairs.

King of Youxian: an honorary title from the Emperor of the Sino-barbarians.

Juyan (and Xiaoguan): please see the footnote for poem 16.

174. Sending Off My Cousin at Lingyun Pool

Lifting a golden glass to drink wine slowly
To the elegant song I listen, tactfully.
The painted boat moves quietly
And the beautiful dance turns round fully.
I sigh for the wagtails separated by the river,
Not following the swans flying over the water.

the wagtail: a Chinese symbol for brother. See also the footnote for poem no. 7.

175. A Joyful Poem for Wang River Villa

This's my house, I live here…
The willow's low branches even brush the ground –
I don't need to sweep it clear,
My pine trees grow vividly, even over the clouds…so tall.
The flower on the rattan looks dull, it disguises some small
Monkey, reaching to hold it near,
And the cypress is just beginning to leaf, all round;
It brings them out, the musk deer…

176. A Poem on the Spot, Meeting Officer Xue Zhou and Murong Sun

To scratch world affairs, keep no sharpness of integrity,
It's a disappearance: all kiss the ground to live.
You guys pay attention to the state of good humanity,
But as for me, definitely I would prefer to give
Myself up to match sweet Heaven's line.
Things from far way, and near, all kind
Of things find their groups and grow up,
End off the earth with exalted standards from Hou Ji;
But pray to Heaven – we must believe in Zhong and Li.
Look, how it is pleased – the spring wind's up!
It even lets me think of the eastern stream…
There the grass's colour, it would seem,
Just appears at the good time, from the warming mud,
And each flower branch contains a tender little bud.
Furthermore, I can await the wonderful scenery coming due,
And take the brilliant green grass to pay my tribute to you.

Hou Ji: the predecessor of the Zhou Dynasty. It is said that his mother stepped on the god of heaven's footprint and then gave birth to him. His mother had given him up so he was also called "Qi," which means given up. During the time of Shun (one of five kings before the Xia Dynasty), he was appointed agricultural officer and taught people how to cultivate crops.

Zhong and Li: Zhong is an ancestor of King Fu Xi, and Li is an ancestor of the He Nation. During the time of Yao (one of the five kings before the Xia Dynasty), they were appointed four-season control officers. They made sure that there were no disturbances between humans and spirits. Each had to concede to the other in his proper sequence.

177. For Li Qi

I heard you like to play the alchemist, drink cinnabar,
So your face would have a simply wonderful colour,
Yet I don't know, from now till you have to leave,
How long you'll have the wings to fly and breathe –
Heaven's wife is hoodwinked by your Hua-Zhi;
I watch you pass the borders of Mount Kunlun.
The immortal beast: the patterned dragon
Following the red leopard one, running over the
10 thousand miles don't even gasp for breath;
How very sad it is: humans, they'd all rather bet on,
Choose, an addiction to the smell of fishy mutton.

Li Qi: a poet in the Tang Dynasty. He used to be a head quarter of county in Xinxiang, Henan province. Later, he resigned and lived a hermit life at Dongchuan Villa close to the east shore of the Ying River. He wrote much poetry and shared friendship with Wang Wei, Gao Shi, and Wang Chang Ling.

Hua-Zhi: a double-meaning word, referring to a royal cart canopy and as well (the alchemists') reishi medicinal mushroom, the "mushroom of immortality."

pattern dragon (Chilong): it said an immortal beast like the dragon and also the unicorn.

Red leopard: said to be an immortal beast, with a leopard's shape, but the body's colour is red. Those are lucky beasts in Chinese mythology.

Mount Kunlun: forms the watershed between the great Yellow and Yangtze rivers, in Xinjiang territory.

The smell of fishy mutton: originally refers the smell of fish and sheep, Wang Wei implies that Li Qi is taking the branch for the root, adding something unnecessary to mainstream culture.

178. After Arriving at Huazhou, I Watch Liyang Across the River, and Recall Ding San's Lodge

From the Huazhou side, I watch the mulberries grow greener and fresher.
The city – Liyang – where I live now surrounds the shining Yellow River.
Look, the life around about here has gone gradually, as it lists,
And here's Mount Dapei, again disappeared in clouds and mists.
Oh, my old friend Ding San, I cannot meet with you right now;
Meanwhile, the Yellow River's still running in a leisurely flow.
For me, the voice of life in Lingyang has also gone somewhere…
Some occasional news, perhaps before long, will spread from there.

Ding San: Wang Wei's friend, who lived in Li Yang as a hermit. Wang Wei lived in Liyang for 3 years before he left to go to Chang An. Ding San made a banquet to send him off, and Wang Wei sent him the poem, "For hermit Ding at the farmhouse."

Huazhou: presently Hua County in Henan Province.

Liyang: an old name for Jun County of Henan Province.

Mt. Dapei: a mountain located in Jun County, Henan Province.

179. For Lay Buddhist Li at Xi River (On the Spot Where I Visit at Master Tan Bi's Temple)

I'm ready to leave, how about you –
Are you really going to follow me?
If I put my heart here, a lotus blooms,
But without putting a heart on a sleeve,
Here will grow the poplar or willow
Wood – how I don't know but it is so.
I will bury the spirit in a pine baldachin,
Into the most healing medicine of Zen.
I will even take a broken stone, you see,
As I can use it as a grinder to grind the tea.
Of course, the taste and smell we both understand –
How is it now I cannot seem to hold your hands?

Lay Buddhist Li: his life was unknown when Wang Wei visited Master Tan Bi's Temple and met him and sent him this poem on the spot.

Xi River: located in Henan province, the Chu culture's cradle.

hold somebody's hands (arm to arm): refers to be one of heart. Wang Wei used this phrase to express that Lay Buddhist Li and he both have a goal to become a Buddhist. Both do the meditation. So they should go to temple (should be converted together).

180. A Gift Poem for My Sixth Uncle, Returning to Luhun

My uncle, your position as a county magistrate at Huaisi, sir,
Has made a great success – if even those good ancient officers
Zhuo Mao and Lu Gong heard it, they would have endorsed it.
It is very leisurely of you to never compete with any others,
And now you return to your hometown to plough as a hermit.
In December, in winter, you trim the mulberry branch;
When the spring winds come, you plant the apricot.
Coming back home, you drink the wine and chance
Making an essay on writing poems, successful or not.
You and I, we can afford to be this gracious,
Knowing that Tao Yuanming was so sagacious.

Luhun: presently the north of Song County in Henan Province.

Huaisi: presently Sishui County in Shandong Province.

Zhuo Mao: an outstanding officer who lived in the East Han Dynasty. He was in harmony with all the people and was very kind. When he was a leader of the country, he reformed the society's atmosphere, to the point where even if you lost something on the road, no one would pick it up.

Lu Gong: a man very similar to Zhuo Mao. When he was a leader of Zhong Mu country, he didn't punish the people. He overcame them by virtue.

Tao Yuanming: (also Tao Qian or Tao Hong Jing) a famous landscape poet in the Eastern Jin and Liu Song Dynasties, considered to be one of the greatest poets of the Six Dynasties period. He used to be a mayor of the county but he tired of the imperial life and resigned to live in seclusion on Mt. Zhong Nan. He liked drinking and he liked willows, planting 5 willow trees by his house. People nicknamed him Mr. Wu Liu (Mr. 5 Willows). His poetry greatly influenced the poets of the Tang Dynasty.

181. A Poem for Prefecture Chief Miao Fengqian at Jinyun

You write a Memorandum to The Throne
To praise the Emperor's sagacity,
And the official seal you wear alone,
As a great officer of full capacity.
You've just arrived at your place, Huiji,
Where the county's head officer is to live
And you wait to meet them, for
A fine horse and cart to you they give –
A Ru Nan Cart from the Emperor,
As a reward for your political success.
When you come back to Songyang,
A suburban area of Jinyun, your horse
And cart running according to the song.
You are walking so slowly, the cymbal sound
Spreads across the whole Qingjiang River.
You have made a big achievement all around
Places like San Wu, where you administer
In your official capacity. All people know you were,
And are, a very valuable man as local head officer.

Prefecture Chief Miao: refers to Miao Fengqian who became a prefecture chief in Jinyun City in Zhejiang Province. When he managed Jinyun, the place achieved peacefulness and prosperity. Immortal music and colourful clouds even appeared on Mt. Jinyun. He reported this phenomenon to Emperor Xuan Zong, who was very happy and invited him to Chang An, and sent him many gifts and a new name for Mt. Jinyun: "Immortal Castle." When he left Chang An, Wang Wei wrote him this poem.

Huiji: Huiji City in Zhejiang Province.

Ru Nan Cart: which means The Emperor's Gifts. This idiom comes from Han Chong, a prefecture chief in Ru Nan County who did such a good job that the Emperor met him and sent him this special cart of many gifts. Later, people made this an idiom meaning gifts from the Emperor.

Jinyun: Lishui City in Zhejiang Province.

Qingjiang River: a river located in the southwest of Hubei Province.

San Wu: indicates the 3 places: Wujun, Wuxing, Huiji, also in Zhejiang Province.

182. Hermit Li Lives on the Mountain

Gentlemen always fill the Emperor's office;
Little people like you would rather choose
To encourage and court, in oneself, success.
You follow the alchemist life style, not to lose;
And you set up your house in the forest,
Beyond the steep summit, as if a test.
It's located at the back of a big hill,
So the flowers haven't bloomed, still.
But the trees reach up towards heaven,
Their colours looking dark or bright,
And throughout the daytime, even,
You still take naps despite the light.
Occasionally a songbird I'm hearing;
On the mountain, it will be twittering.

183. The Morning I Entered Xingyang City

That morning, into Xingze our boat began to pull,
And I realized this city was so vital and powerful.
The river zigzagged through the streets and village lanes,
And along the water, cooking smoke drifted in long trains.
I met the local people, observed the local customs;
Entering the docks, heard dialects of local persons.
The autumn fields stretched far, full of thriving crops –
Once the morning shines, the market noise won't stop.
The fish dealer had become the waves' personal guest;
Cocks and dogs standing by the village were impressed.
The future's road is very far from here, in the white cloud;
Right now I drive the single and lonely boat, as allowed,
But what will my future be, I wondered? It's unguessed.

Xingze: an old lake in Xingyang and Xingze counties in Henan Province.

184. Crossing the Yellow River to Qinghe

I boat on the Yellow River – the river so huge,
Even heaven connects to this enormous water.
Suddenly, the remote place – where the hues
Of blue water and heaven connect and alter –
Together open a gap, and there! The many pretty
Households, castles and villages, running along
With the river…again I can see the town or city.
It seems as if the suburbs are where mulberries belong.
I look back: will my old hometown these visions bring?
I only can see the river, the rosy clouds, connecting,
Drifting apart, drifting together, aimlessly…drifting.

185. The Willow's Waves *(Wang River Collection)*

Your slender form separates into two wavy lines
Of beautiful willows, highs and then lows,
And your shadow in the lake reflects, realigns.
You don't learn to estimate the other willows…
They grow up by the Yu-Gou, an imperial river.
When the spring wind blows, they become
A keepsake to break off and a somewhat clever
Expression in wounded leaves, for some.

The Willow's Waves: one of the 20 sites on the Wang River where Wang Wei lived.

186. Pepper Plantation

Lifting a jar of the finest osmanthus wine now,
To welcome Di-Zi, the daughter of King Yao,
Procuring the pallia japonica plant, with a plan
To afterwards present it to a beautiful woman…
None one of these can compare to –
Sitting upon a very smooth mat
And putting your best peppers into
A coarse wine, a sacrifice that
Expects the cloud god coming through.

Pepper Plantation: one of the 20 sites on the Wang River where Wang Wei lived.

Di-Zi: Lady Xiang – rumoured to be a daughter of King Yao.

A cloud god: it was believed that a god administers the weather's changes, such as wind, clouds, rain, thunder, lightning.

187. Osprey Weir *(Poems at Huangpu Yue's Yunxi Villa)*

Suddenly your body buries into the red lotus,
Then your wings appear from the green rush-straw.
With dripping wings, you stand as if for us,
On an old raft, fetching the fish up for your craw.

188. Shangping Field *(Poems at Huangpu Yue's Yunxi Villa)*

In the morning you cultivate Shangping field,
In the evening you cultivate Shangping field.
May I ask for somebody who makes inquiries as if for wages,
How do you know that Chang Ju and Jie Ni are both sages?

Chang Ju and Jie Ni: this idiom comes from "The Analects of Confucius." They are not names of persons; they represent two typical characters. Chang Ju is a tall man; Jie Ni is a strong fat man. Later, people take this idiom to represent hermits.

189. Duckweed *(Poems at Huangpu Yue's Yunxi Villa)*

In Spring the pool grows full of duckweed.
When the boat comes back along the lee,
The duckweed separated by its outbound speed
Has by then drawn together and closed tightly.
But then afterwards and for a while the dance
Of the wind blowing many a low-hanging branch
Of the willow trees, or poplars, freely,
Sweeping the surface of the water just by chance…
The duckweed opens up just as surely.

190. I Heard Pei Di Made Poems – Then I Sent Him this Joyful Poem

How hard it is – the apes sing
With sorrow in the morning
And sadness in the evening.
I would like to tell you:
Please do not make a sound
Like apes at Wuxia do –
That can cause the guests around
The river in autumn to need relief,
Or to be overwhelmed by grief.

Wuxia (Wu Gorge): one of the Three Gorges, bound on the west by the Da Ning River in Wushan County, and Chongqing City in Sichuan Province, and on the east by the Guandu River in Badong county in Hubei Province. Its famous deeper beauty shines on both sides: there are 12 summits. One of the summits is called Immortal Maiden, said to be an embodiment of the immortal maiden who helped Yu control the water. Its length is 45 kilometres.

191. The Portrait of Cui Xingzong.

I painted your portrait when you were young
Years later, right now, you're getting older
There are new people that I am among…
And so I understand how it's much better
That you're an old friend I made before.

your portrait: Wang Wei was also a famous painter.

192. Suspicious Dream

Please do not be surprised to meet
Your favourite thing or a special defeat,
Humiliation or an empty joy,
Or dreams that worry and annoy.
Please do not care for grace or hate –
That is all a sad, laborious waste.
Where can I ask about who was
The King of Yellow or Confucius?
How to know? They probably became
A drifting dreamboat in my dream.

The King of Yellow: The Yellow Emperor. The footnote at poem 43 explains more.

193. To Send Off Officer Li to Dongjiang

You will be the envoy to Dongjiang, I hear, for sure;
There the local people will follow you, imperial officer.
You will send wax-sealed memoranda to the throne
That report your insights on the local situation –
This mission will chiefly rest on you alone
And there you will moralize this tattooing nation.
Every day you will enjoy the greens at the Yangtze River
And observe the tides of the Fu Chun with pleasure.
I feel I know that you will go to this time and place
To collect pearls and precious stones for the Emperor.
I believe you will bring the Emperor's special grace
To the fortunate one who is the local pearl breeder.

Officer Li: an adjutant to the mayor.

Dongjiang: a region located in Hunan Province, rich in pearls, in Ancient China.

tattooing nation: indicates an uncivilized barbarian horde.

precious stones: this indicates the precious stones of He Shi, from a story coming from the book, *Han Fei Zi*. A man called Bian He found a precious stone and offered it to two of the kings of Chu (Li and Wu), but they disbelieved his story and each king cut off one of his legs, leaving him crippled. Then a third king (Wen) heard that Bian He still kept the precious stone and was still crying on Mount Chu. He sent an officer to ask why. The officer reported that Bian He told him that the reason he kept crying was that everyone believed his precious stone to be only another common stone. So the king asked one of his workers to cut open the "common" stone – then an invaluable jade was revealed!

pearl breeder: this creature is very similar to a mermaid; she lived in the south sea of China, her lower body like a fish. Her tears could transform into pearls. Also, a worker in the pearl business!

194. Sending Off Zhang Wu (Yin) to Xuancheng

You'll travel far, ten thousand miles away –
It is that far, the region of Five Lakes.
And to reach the place where you will stay,
To journey west of that is what it takes.
Nan Ling Castle's found close to the shore,
Households settle by the valley stream.
You will want to come back more and more –
The river's like a huge and boundless dream –
You'll see the grass sprout up along your route,
Grow tall and start to ripple in the wind
And still you've not arrived, still in pursuit
Of Lanling town – the place where you'll begin
Official work. And there you'll hear the hoots
And moaning from the apes in those locales,
Though that's the place your consciousness escapes
Having to hear the sighs of Chang An pals
Bearing heavy official burdens beneath fine capes.

Five lakes: indicates 5 freshwater lakes in China: Dongting (in Hunan Province), Poyang (in Jiangxi Province), Chao (In Anhui Province), Hongze Lake (in Hubei Province), and Tai Lake (in Jiangsu Province).

Lanling: an ancient place between in Jiangsu and Anhui. Its wine gained great fame in Ancient China.

195. Sending Off He Sui's Nephew

Now you'll boat down to the south;
The boat will travel upstream of Jingmen.
Beside the reeds, it is uncouth;
Beside the silver grass, it's gloomy when?
Most of the time, and the river's length is long.
The King, Chu Shao's, tomb's long hid among
The clouds and water you will sail again,
One spar with a crow from far Chang An.
And in the evening returns the chill rain –
You watch the river fill, as it's raining on,
And on. You're liable to get sorrowful.
You'd be better off to reach your destination
Before Mt. Chu's autumn, sad and dull.
The apes cry then, and hurt one's imagination.

Jingmen: this refers to Jingmen City in Hubei Province.

Chu Shao's tomb: a tomb of the King of Shao in Chu State.

Mt. Chu: rises in the west of Hubei Province, southeast of Mt. Wu Dang. It's a very famous scenic spot: the rock is very rich in jade. It is said that Bian He obtained precious stones there. Please see footnote for poem 193 about Bian He.

196. Sending Qiwu Qian Home After He Fails His State Examination

There's not much lack, when now the Emperor is a sage,
Of heroes coming out to serve the state. It's a new page –
Even you, living like a monk close to the Eastern Mount,
No longer considered picking up the vetches roundabout,
And came into town to take the official exam of state.
But you failed – now you must depart the golden gate
Of government acceptance. Do you think things are going
All that wrong? Now a new season's arriving, of growing;
The Hanshi festivals in southern Jianghuai are now underway,
Though at northern Luoyang and Chang An they still, they say,
Are sewing their spring dresses with skill and care.
Although you are getting a goodbye banquet here,
I know that you and I will always miss each other.
You'll be sailing away on the boat which you now await,
But eventually you will get to open your hometown gate;
There the district jungles will hide your shadow; the late
Setting sun on the old castle will shine, intense…
It's just that you weren't hired – it's no offence.
Please don't sigh about having less influence.

A hermit close to the Eastern Mount: in the Eastern Jin Dynasty, Xie An was living in solitude on the Eastern Mountain (in Huiji City in Zhejiang Province) so famously that this location became a metaphor for hermit life.

picking up the vetches: this story's from the Zhou Dynasty – two men, Wei Zi and Qi Zi, used to be Marquis in the Shang Dynasty. After Shang died, they tried to live on Mt. Shou Yang, picking vetches to support their lives, as in those footnotes for poems 157 and 43. They finally died of starvation.

golden gate: a place where the Emperor met the new officers (also called "the golden horse gate"). It represents passing the state examination and becoming an official.

Hanshi festival: a festival deriving from a story of the Spring and Autumn period. Before Zhong Er (a King of Jin State) became a King, he was exiled in other countries. His secretary, Jie Zhitui, followed him devotedly, even, when they were starving, cutting some meat from his own leg to feed Zhong Er. After Zhong Er became a King, Jie Zhitui didn't accept the King's grace, but went with his mother to a secluded mountain to live there humbly. The very determined King then burnt this mountain to force him out, but Jie Zhitui was killed in the fire. In memory of him, the King ordered that day to be a day in Jin when all fires – even cooking fires – were prohibited.

197. Hua Zi Gang *(Wang River Collection)*

For these birds I can’t account, they’re flying round and round;
I first surmount and then descend the long hill of Hua Zi Gang.
They must wear autumn colours now, the mountains that surround.
My Fall years come; my mood’s obscure, its melancholy, strong.

198. Jinzhu Hill *(Wang River Collection)*

I seek a place to meditate…somewhere vast, somewhere remote.
In these pretty bamboo-forest forms the carefree wind will show,
Their green and tender ripples flow like waves beneath my boat.
The woods slip onto the Shang Shan Road; even there they'd go;
My secret retreat, even diligent monk woodcutters will not know.

Shangshan: a mountain in Shang County in Shaanxi Province. It can also represent a hermit. The mountain's shape is very similar to the Chinese character "Shang" and so it got named Shangshan or, Mount Shang.

199. Sending Off Officer Yang to Guozhou

The road to Bao and Xie, strategic and so narrow,
Is difficult to travel down, even with a cart.
How is it a difficult place, where you must go?
The advantageous road – for birds, in part,
Extends far along there, over ten miles long;
On both sides of the cliffs, apes are crying
From day to night, singing the saddest song.
By the government bridge, fortune-telling
Wizards offer to reveal to you your fate
And ritual priests pour libations for you.
In the old forests, ancient temples await
Where they pray the goddess will come through.
Although we'll be apart, we both can watch
The same moon's long rise and fall, and listen to
The cuckoo's song, whose melody will touch
Our hearts, and for your return you'll long anew.

The road to Bao and Xie: an ancient road, its name taken from the two valleys it connects, Bao and Xie.

Cuckoo's song: it was said that after the old State of Shu was destroyed by the State of Qin, the King of Shu became a cuckoo, crying every day.

200. Dogwood

Under the mountain, dogwood blooms,
Its fragrance stronger in the cold.
Through the windows of my little room
I see them with their friends of old,
Osmanthus, facing the autumnal moon.

Dogwood: Please see the footnote No.7 and 174.

POSTSCRIPT

Last spring I returned to China due to problems with my parents' tomb. After settling things at the cemetery, I went to Wang River with local poet Mrs. Zhang Kaili and her friends. Wang River is a remote place, and if it weren't for Mrs. Kaili, I wouldn't have been able to find it.

This visit resulted in "A Song to Wang River."

A Song to Wang River

Lean on Qi Lake and it will drip many jade beads,
Accompany Mount Yao and run clear with seeds.
The stream zigzags as if a spoked wheel radiating,
The path being circuitous, a magic ring drifting.
I don't know when Wang River was born
But I can see its beautiful shape has gone.
I know Wang River was created in ancient times, but
It became famous due to only one person – the poet,
Wang Wei.
The bright moon shines among the pine woods;
The clear stream runs around our green boat.
Mr. Song Zhi Wen's old villa, he had bought
And built a marvellous home for his many moods,
Invited his friend Mr. Pei Di, cultivated the calamus cushion,
Toured the mountain and river, a duty of the officer position,
Played the white lyre, mused around the poetic layer,
Listened to the birds twittering, worked up the Zen breathing.
The 20 landscapes of the Wang River come from Wang Wei;
Over 100 of the poems by Wang Wei to the Wang River relate.
The King of Liu Bang passed by Jin Zhu Hill in the time of Han,
And left the song of a phoenix, that special song in China
And in the Tang Dynasty Wang Wei lived on Mount Zhong Nan
And built a deer thicket and got a unique copy of River Ba.

Look around the River Wang: in front of the ragged house standing,
With the unique ginkgo shaking, the rugged mountain embracing
The village with no clear river or lake, and no birds twittering.

At the back of the highway, the railway runs through the hill
On which sits no commemorative block of stone, or any will.
On the left side, a stone cave has opened and you sight
Wang Wei's figure in stone – it shines in the setting sun.
The simple stream in this vicinity also reflects the light.
And this light even radiates upon the green mountain.
The right side is the one the stores are lined upon,
And guests' voices disturb the quiet River Wang.
Sadly, at today's Wang River, there's no evidence,
Only a ginkgo tree that was planted, in a sense,
By his breathing-writing, with some ancient tablets.
Sadly, old Mount Zhong Nan has no hermit tests,
And lacks all the alchemy with a half-crystal content.
When I watched the present Wang River before I went,
I couldn't help writing a poem to express my discontent.

I make light of travelling from a far place – Canada;
I want to see the traces of the temple covered
By a new bamboo woods in the Wang River area.
However, in the new Wang River watershed,
I find the clear stream of Wang River has gone.
And only in its branches float the clouds.
Although its basic outline does still zigzag on.
Sitting and appreciating the unique boughs
Of the ginkgo tree that was painted by Wang Wei,
Thinking of, remembering, the Deer Thicket lines
That were printed when the Tang Dynasty held sway,
I wish to see a new colour replace the present Sign –
In the gully where birds twitter their return today.

left to right: Liu Yuankai, Zhang Kaili, David Du, Liu Huancun

Manufactured by Amazon.ca
Bolton, ON

17881487R00140